THE SALEM
WITCH TRIALS

MILESTONES
IN AMERICAN HISTORY

THE ACQUISITION OF FLORIDA

THE ALAMO

ALEXANDER GRAHAM BELL
AND THE TELEPHONE

THE ATTACK ON PEARL HARBOR

THE BOSTON TEA PARTY

THE CALIFORNIA GOLD RUSH

THE CIVIL RIGHTS ACT OF 1964

THE CUBAN MISSILE CRISIS

THE DONNER PARTY

THE ELECTRIC LIGHT

THE EMANCIPATION PROCLAMATION

THE ERIE CANAL

THE GREAT BLACK MIGRATION

THE GREAT DEPRESSION
AND THE NEW DEAL

THE INTERNMENT OF
JAPANESE AMERICANS
DURING WORLD WAR II

THE INVENTION OF
THE MOVING ASSEMBLY LINE

THE LOUISIANA PURCHASE

MANIFEST DESTINY

THE MCCARTHY ERA

THE MONROE DOCTRINE

THE OREGON TRAIL

THE OUTBREAK OF THE CIVIL WAR

THE PONY EXPRESS

THE PROHIBITION ERA

THE RAID ON HARPERS FERRY

THE ROBBER BARONS AND THE
SHERMAN ANTITRUST ACT

THE SALEM WITCH TRIALS

THE SCOPES MONKEY TRIAL

THE SINKING OF THE USS *MAINE*

SPUTNIK/EXPLORER I

THE STOCK MARKET CRASH OF 1929

THE TRANSCONTINENTAL RAILROAD

THE TREATY OF PARIS

THE UNDERGROUND RAILROAD

THE WRIGHT BROTHERS

THE SALEM WITCH TRIALS

HYSTERIA IN COLONIAL AMERICA

LOUISE CHIPLEY SLAVICEK

CHELSEA HOUSE
An Infobase Learning Company

The Salem Witch Trials

Copyright © 2011 by Infobase Learning

Chelsea House
An imprint of Infobase Learning
132 West 31st Street
New York, NY 10001

Library of Congress Cataloging-in-Publication Data

Slavicek, Louise Chipley, 1956-
The Salem witchcraft trials / by Louise Chipley Slavicek.
    p. cm. — (Milestones in American history)
Includes bibliographical references and index.
ISBN 978-1-60413-763-7 (hardcover)
1. Trials (Witchcraft)—Massachusetts—Salem—Juvenile literature. 2. Witchcraft—Massachusetts—Salem—History—Juvenile literature. I. Title.

KFM2478.8.W5S59 2011
133.4'3097445—dc22   2011002489

Chelsea House books are available at special discounts when purchased in bulk quantities for businesses, associations, institutions, or sales promotions. Please call our Special Sales Department in New York at (212) 967-8800 or (800) 322-8755.

You can find Chelsea House on the World Wide Web at http://www.infobaselearning.com.

Text design by Erik Lindstrom
Cover design by Alicia Post
Composition by Keith Trego
Cover printed by Yurchak Printing, Landisville, Pa.
Book printed and bound by Yurchak Printing, Landisville, Pa.
Date printed: July 2011
Printed in the United States of America

10 9 8 7 6 5 4 3 2 1

This book is printed on acid-free paper.

All links and Web addresses were checked and verified to be correct at the time of publication. Because of the dynamic nature of the Web, some addresses and links may have changed since publication and may no longer be valid.

CONTENTS

1 Introduction 1

2 Witchcraft in the Old and New Worlds 5

3 On the Eve of the Salem Witchcraft Crisis 19

4 The Accusations Begin 32

5 The First Trials 47

6 A Deadly Panic 60

7 Growing Doubts 75

8 Aftermath and Legacy 88

Chronology 101

Timeline 102

Notes 104

Bibliography 107

Further Reading 109

Photo Credits 111

Index 112

About the Author 119

Introduction

Sometime during the early winter of 1692, Betty Parris and Abigail Williams, two young residents of the quiet Massachusetts hamlet of Salem Village, started to act very peculiarly. Both girls lived in the household of Samuel Parris, the Puritan minister of the village's only church. Nine-year-old Betty was Parris's daughter and 11-year-old Abigail, his niece. To Reverend Parris's consternation, the girls, who had always appeared perfectly healthy and well adjusted, suddenly began to suffer mysterious fits. They rolled on the floor, shrieking and writhing. They made horrible rasping noises as though they were being choked. Sometimes they crawled around the house on their hands and knees, barking and growling like dogs. Other times they cowered in corners or under the furniture, insisting that invisible attackers were biting them or jabbing them with pins.

Perplexed and frightened by the girls' bizarre behavior, Parris asked a local physician to examine them. After ruling out a medical cause for their odd symptoms, the doctor made an alarming diagnosis. Betty and Abigail, he declared, were "under an evil hand."[1] In other words, they had fallen victim to Satan's earthly agents—witches. Pressured by Parris to name their witch tormenters, the girls identified three local women, including the Parris family's West Indian slave. So began what would quickly escalate into the largest, deadliest, and most famous witch hunt in American history, the Salem witchcraft crisis of 1692–1693.

WITCHCRAFT IN PURITAN NEW ENGLAND

Just about everyone in Puritan Massachusetts—educated and uneducated, young and old alike—believed in the existence of diabolical witchcraft (witchcraft influenced by the devil). English Puritans had fled religious persecution in their homeland and first settled the region 70 years earlier. They and their ancestors, observes historian Larry Gragg, "inhabited a mental world that few in this century would recognize. It often was a frightening place, one in which individuals suffered assaults from agents of the 'invisible world.'"[2] (By "invisible world," Puritan New Englanders meant the supernatural realm.) If unexpected misfortune struck a family or community—children or livestock suddenly fell sick, crops failed, barns caught fire—people automatically assumed that witchcraft was to blame. Consequently, when the doctor suggested that Betty and Abigail were "under an evil hand," most Salem villagers accepted his diagnosis.

Yet, while diabolical witchcraft was widely feared in New England in 1692, relatively few New Englanders had actually been convicted of it. Prior to the outbreak of the Salem witch craze, approximately 100 New England colonists had been charged with practicing witchcraft. Of that total, only about one-fifth were found guilty and 14 executed.

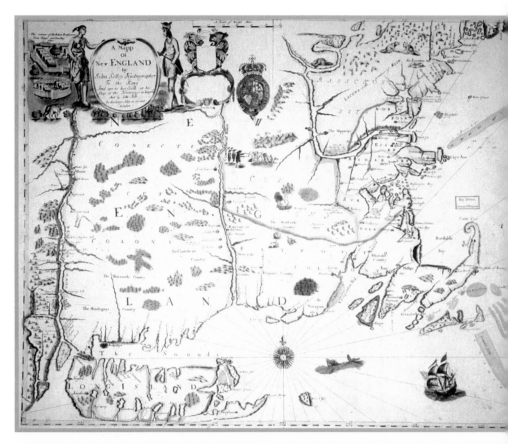

A map of colonial New England, circa 1675.

The Salem witchcraft panic marked a dramatic break with New England's previously cautious approach to convicting and punishing reputed witches. Although the Salem episode lasted for less than a year, by the time it was over at least 155 witch suspects had been hauled off to jail; 19 convicted witches had been hanged; and one man had been crushed to death for refusing to stand trial. Over the years, scholars have hotly debated the reasons for the unprecedented scale and intensity of the Salem witchcraft crisis, helping to make it among the best-known and most widely studied events in American history. While we may never know why the Salem crisis unfolded as it did, one thing is certain: The deadly Massachusetts witch hunt has left an enduring imprint on American culture and society. Even today, more than three centuries later, the Salem persecutions serve as a stark reminder to Americans of the perils of intolerance and fear-driven trials.

Witchcraft in the Old and New Worlds

T he roots of the Salem witchcraft trials go back thousands of years to biblical times. Virtually all the ancient peoples of the Middle East believed in the existence of witches, including the Hebrew founders of the Jewish religion. "Thou shalt not suffer a witch to live," admonishes the book of Exodus of the Hebrew Bible (the Old Testament to Christians).[1] Later in the Bible, God commands the Hebrews: "There shall not be found among you anyone. . . that useth . . . an enchanter or a witch."[2]

WITCHCRAFT AND THE CATHOLIC CHURCH

During the first century A.D., the leaders of the new Christian religion incorporated the Hebrew Bible's extremely negative view of witchcraft into their own faith. Like the Hebrews, the early Christians never doubted that witches were real or that their supernatural powers came from the "prince of darkness" himself, Satan. Also in common with their Jewish brethren, Christians assumed "humans had the ability to ally themselves with either side of the great spiritual struggle between God and Satan," observes historian K. David Goss. "Those who . . . voluntarily associated themselves with the forces of spiritual darkness by calling upon satanic powers to harm others . . . were regarded as 'witches' and spiritual enemies of the church," he writes.[3]

Despite their contempt for witchcraft, for centuries following the establishment of the first Christian churches in the Middle East and southern Europe, Christian leaders made little effort to seek out and punish suspected witches. By the High Middle Ages (1000 to 1300 A.D.), the Roman Catholic Church had become the dominant religious and social organization throughout most of the European continent. During this period, local Catholic officials occasionally tried reputed witches on charges of heresy (a belief that differs from a religion's orthodox creed). But it was not until well into the Late Middle Ages (1300 to 1500) that the opposition of the top Catholic leadership toward witches began to harden, and the church started to hunt down and prosecute them in large numbers.

A major turning point in the Catholic Church's attitude toward witch hunting took place during the late 1400s. In 1484, the head of the Roman Catholic Church, Pope Innocent VIII, issued a formal proclamation condemning witchcraft as devil worship, the worst of all heresies, and called on church and civil authorities to use harsher measures against anyone suspected of practicing it. Three years later, Innocent allowed his anti-witchcraft proclamation to be used as the preface to the first major book on witchcraft, *Malleus Maleficarum*, or *The Hammer of Witches*. Written by two monks, Heinrich Kramer and Jacob Sprenger, *Malleus Maleficarum* gave specific guidelines to church and secular (nonreligious) officials for discovering and convicting witches, whom the authors por-

INNOCENTIO OTTAVO.   219

INNOCENTIVS·PP·VIII LIGVR

Pope Innocent VIII (*above*) condemned witchcraft as devil worship in 1484. His proclamation called on authorities to punish harshly anyone who practiced it.

trayed as powerful and savagely cruel. Kramer and Sprenger's sensationalistic book described in colorful detail the evil deeds of witches, including baby killing and cannibalism. It also warned ominously of the existence of a large, organized cult of witches that all Christians had a sacred obligation to uncover and destroy.

EUROPE'S WITCH CRAZE

Between 1487 and 1520, *Malleus Maleficarum* would be reprinted 13 times and become one of the most widely read books in Europe, serving as "a virtual bible of witch-hunting," according to historian John Demos.[4] Even the Reformation, the sixteenth-century religious movement that led to the founding of the Protestant churches, did not take away from the book's appeal among European Christians. Although written by two Catholic monks and authorized by the pope, *Malleus Maleficarum* was as popular in Protestant regions as in those that remained loyal to the Catholic Church. "Belief in witchcraft, witches, Satan, and the spiritual powers of good and evil were no less real to . . . Protestants than to their Roman Catholic counterparts," contends Goss.[5] Both groups understood witchcraft as a contract by which an individual agreed to serve the devil in return for supernatural powers. New witches supposedly formalized their evil pact with Satan by signing the "devil's book," listing all the women and men recruited as witches or wizards, as male witches were sometimes called.

By the mid-1500s, deepening popular anxiety about witchcraft, and particularly the large underground witch cult described in *Malleus Maleficarum*, had ripened into what has come to be known as the great European witch craze. Witchcraft trials increased substantially throughout most of Europe, and the use of torture to obtain confessions became common. Aside from confessions, witches were identified by a number of different tests, including the notorious water test, in which the accused was thrown into deep water after her thumbs had been tied to her toes. If she sank, she was judged to be innocent of witchcraft; if she stayed afloat, she was guilty. A more common test was pricking the skin of a suspected witch with pins. Supposedly, all witches had a "devil's mark" somewhere on their bodies that was insensitive to pain and served as a sign of their secret pact with Satan.

No one can say with certainty how many innocent women and men became victims of the European witchcraft frenzy. But according to some estimates, at least 100,000 persons were tried for witchcraft and 50,000–60,000 executed between 1550 and 1650, when the craze finally began to die down. Historians have noted that the violence and scope of the European witch hunts tended to increase during times of political, religious, and economic turmoil. "Yet inflation, depression, poor harvests, rumors of war, or hostilities between Catholics and Protestants would not necessarily trigger a search for witches," maintains author Larry Gragg. "The most likely locales of rigorous hunts were those that experienced some of the above conditions in conjunction with an intense fear of a powerful witch conspiracy," he writes.[6]

Gragg's observation regarding the most common places for the deadliest witch hunts may explain why England, the Massachusetts Puritans' native land, experienced the witch craze of the mid-sixteenth to mid-seventeenth centuries on a significantly smaller scale than most other western European countries. An estimated 1,500 to 2,000 suspected witches were tried in English courts between 1550 and 1650, and about 300 were ultimately convicted and executed by hanging. (In the rest of Europe, convicted witches were usually burned at the stake rather than hanged.) "Restraint in the use of judicial coercion partly explains the comparatively low figures," notes Gragg. "Most crucial, however, was the focus of English trials. Judges displayed little concern for the discovery of an organized witch society," he argues.[7] Although they would have been familiar with Kramer and Sprenger's claims regarding a vast, secret cult of devil worshippers, few civil authorities in England seem to have taken them seriously. Rather, English judges focused on the issue of *maleficium*, the specific harm that witches allegedly caused to other people. For example, accused witches were often brought to trial on charges they had caused a neighbor's child to sicken and die or a harvest to fail. Supposedly, witches committed these malevolent acts because they were consumed by jealousy and a cruel desire to makes others suffer. Therefore, when an unexpected misfortune struck a family or an entire village, it was often blamed on any community members suspected of practicing witchcraft.

WOMEN AND THE GREAT EUROPEAN WITCH HUNTS

In England and throughout most of Europe, an estimated 80 percent of accused witches were female. Over the centuries since the witch craze, historians have struggled to explain this striking statistic. "A witch could at least in theory as easily be male as female," observes John Demos.[8] In practice, however, women were far more likely to be seen as witches.

Sixteenth- and seventeenth-century European women lived in a highly patriarchal (male-dominated) society. Men were the recognized heads of household, owned most of the property, and held virtually all the religious, legal, and political power. Misogyny—the hatred of women—was also common in the popular culture of the period. *Malleus Maleficarum* was deeply misogynist in tone, blaming the existence of witchcraft chiefly on the "wickedness" and intellectual inferiority of women. Wrote Kramer and Sprenger: "All wickedness is but little to the wickedness of a woman. . . .Women are easily provoked to hatred. . . .They are credulous; and since the chief aim of the Devil is to corrupt faith, therefore he rather attacks them. . . . Since they are feebler both in mind and body, it is not surprising that they should come more under the spell of witchcraft."[9]

Yet to characterize the great European witch craze as simply "an attack on women . . . leaves several problems unexplained," writes historian Robert Thurston.[10] For one thing, females made up a majority of the accusers as well as a majority of the accused in many parts of Europe. A "women-against-women

During most of the sixteenth and seventeenth centuries in Europe, women were more likely than men to be accused of being witches. This illustration shows three alleged female witches being burned alive in Switzerland.

dynamic was fundamental to many witchcraft cases, especially those playing out at the village level," Demos observes.[11] For another, neither male political, religious, and economic dominance over women nor misogyny was new in the Late Middle Ages and early Modern Era. They had been present to one degree or another in European society and culture long before the witchcraft frenzy developed. Indeed, the commonly held attitude during the sixteenth and seventeenth centuries that women were more vulnerable to Satan's influence was rooted in the ancient scriptures. According to the Bible, it was the fickleness of the first woman, Eve, that brought about humankind's "fall" from the Garden of Eden after she gave into Satan's urgings and disobeyed God by eating the fruit of the Tree of Life. During late antiquity (about 250–600 A.D.) and the early Middle Ages, church leaders enthusiastically took up the theme of women's guilt and moral frailty from the Hebrew Bible, even though the church rarely prosecuted alleged witches during this period. For example, in a particularly misogynistic address, the

A DISCOURSE ON THE DAMNED ART OF WITCHCRAFT

The best-known English work on witchcraft published during the era of the great European witch craze was by a Puritan clergyman, William Perkins. Published in London in 1608, Perkins's *A Discourse of the Damned Art of Witchcraft, So Far Forth as It Is Revealed in the Scriptures and Manifest by True Experience*, was even more widely read in Puritan-ruled New England than in England, where Puritans were in the minority.

Perkins's discussion of the typical characteristics of a witch in Chapter 5 of his discourse reflects the standard contemporary view of females as morally and intellectually inferior to males, and therefore more likely to fall under Satan's sway. In the chapter, he also calls for harsh punishment for all convicted witches, regardless of their gender:

What witches be, and of how many sorts:
A witch is a magician, who either by open or secret league, wittingly and willingly, contenteth to use the aid and assistance of the Devil, in the working of wonders.

early Christian patriarch Tertullian asked his female listeners: "And do you know that you are [each] an Eve? . . . You are the Devil's gateway. You are the unsealer of that (forbidden) tree."[12]

Aside from being female, a majority of accused witches during the European witch craze shared two other traits: Most of the suspected witches were poor, and most were middle-aged (approximately 40 to 60 years of age). People of wealth and high social standing were rarely brought to trial on witchcraft charges. Older women—and less often older men—were considerably more likely to become targets of witch hunts

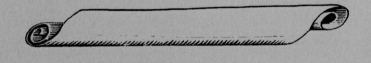

. . . the woman being the weaker sex, is sooner entangled by the Devil's illusions with this damnable art, than the man. And in all ages it is found true by experience that the Devil hath more easily and oftener prevailed with women, than with men. Hence it was, that the Hebrews of ancient times, used it for a proverb, The more women, the more witches. . . .

Secondly, to take away all exception of punishment from any party that shall practice this trade, and to show that weakness cannot exempt the witch from death. For in all reason, if any might allege infirmity, and plead for favour, it were the woman, who is weaker than the man. But the Lord saith, if any person of either sex among his people, be found to have entered covenant with Satan, and become a practiser of sorcery; though it be a woman and the weaker vessel, she shall not escape, she shall not be suffered to live. . . .

* Quoted in Frances Hill, *The Salem Witchcraft Trials Reader.* New York: Da Capo Press, 2000, p. 6.

than younger people, perhaps became they had had more years to establish a reputation in their communities for odd or contentious behavior.

DIFFERING APPROACHES TO WITCHCRAFT IN THE AMERICAN COLONIES

When English colonists began settling in North America during the early seventeenth century, they naturally brought their belief in witchcraft with them from the Old World. In Virginia and the other southern colonies, as well as in New York, after it came under English rule in 1664, colonial laws regarding witchcraft generally mirrored those in England. Thus, the colonies' legal codes focused on *maleficium*—the specific harm that witches did to their victims—rather than the witches' offenses against God as alleged Satan worshippers. In the southern and middle colonies, however, judges were less likely to convict people of witchcraft than in England, where considerably fewer witches were executed than in most other western European countries during the late medieval and early modern periods.

Throughout the colonial period, New York had no executions for witchcraft and only a handful of witchcraft trials. Pennsylvania, which neglected to pass any witchcraft laws until the early eighteenth century, tried just one woman for witchcraft, and she was found innocent. In Virginia, only one individual was convicted of witchcraft in the colony's courts, and he was exiled rather than executed for his alleged crime. Virginia authorities worried that "charges of sorcery posed an enormous potential for gross miscarriages of justice," contends historian Thomas Purvis. Consequently, in 1655, the colonial assembly approved harsh penalties for any Virginian who indulged in "slander and scandal" by falsely labeling others as witches. "Numerous individuals won lawsuits alleging defamation of character under the 1655 law, for Virginia courts invariably responded with a healthy dose of skepticism toward accusations of sorcery," Purvis writes.[13]

The history of witchcraft took a very different path in the early New England colonies. Unlike the legal codes of the southern and middle colonies, New England's witchcraft statutes were firmly grounded in the Old Testament, and accused witches were vigorously prosecuted not only for *maleficium* but also for their sins against God and religion. By the standards of the rest of British America, New England's Puritan authorities were exceptionally diligent in hunting down and trying suspected witches. According to some estimates, more than 100 women and men were tried as witches in New England courts before the Salem witchcraft trials began in 1692. New Englanders were more likely to bring witches to trial by the standards of their native land as well as those of their colonial neighbors. Since far fewer people lived in the region than in England during the seventeenth century, when considered in relation to their total populations, "indictments for witchcraft were 25 times more frequent in New England than in the mother country," observes Purvis.[14]

WITCHCRAFT AND THE PURITANS' NEW WORLD MISSION

Historians agree that the New Englanders' Puritan religious beliefs played a central role in the substantial gap between the numbers of witches brought to trial in New England and in other parts of British North America, even before the Salem witch hysteria of the early 1690s began. Puritanism first took root in New England in 1620, when a small group of Separatist Puritans—the Pilgrims—founded the Plymouth Colony in what is today southern Massachusetts. Ten years later, a much larger group of Puritan colonists established the Massachusetts Bay Colony just north of Plymouth, with the port town of Boston as its political center. Puritanism had first developed in England during the mid-1500s, after King Henry VIII split with the Roman Catholic Church and declared the new Anglican Communion as his kingdom's state church. Although the Anglican Communion was technically Protestant, many of its rituals and teachings still closely resembled those of the Roman Catholic Church. As a result, some English religious reformers believed their country's Protestant Reformation had not gone far enough. The disgruntled reformers soon came to be known as Puritans because of their desire to "purify" Anglicanism of all remnants of Catholic practice and doctrine. A small number of Puritans, like the Pilgrims of Plymouth Bay, evolved into Separatists, meaning that they gave up all hope of changing the Anglican Church from within and wanted to separate completely from it. Most Puritans, like the large group who settled Massachusetts Bay, clung to the hope that the Anglican leadership would one day see the light and concede to their demands. In their theology, all Puritans followed the harsh teachings of the Protestant reformer, John Calvin, who emphasized the absolute sinfulness of mankind and the absolute righteousness of God.

A desire to escape growing persecution from Anglican authorities was a key motivating factor behind the Puritan migration to New England beginning in the second decade of the 1600s. Of equal importance in spurring the Puritans to forsake their homeland for the American wilderness was the emigrants' vision of creating a model Christian community in the New World. The Puritans were convinced they had a sacred mission to create a new kind of society in the New England wilderness, one that was firmly grounded in their strict religious and moral principles. If the Puritans all worked together to fulfill their God-given mission, their new community would be, in the words of Massachusetts's first governor, John Winthrop, a "city upon a hill," a refuge for the one "true" faith and a beacon of spiritual light for the rest of humankind to follow.[15] Because of the holy nature of their New World undertaking, the Puritans worried that God's archenemy, Satan, wanted their mission to fail just as much as the Almighty wanted it to succeed. To prevent the devil from destroying their God-fearing city upon a hill, the New Englanders believed they must remain

Puritan colonists believed that it was their mission to create a refuge for like-minded worshippers in the New World. They were wary of anything that seemed to be a result of Satan's influence, which they thought was exercised through witchcraft.

constantly vigilant in defending their faith and community from Satan's harmful influence, including the evil power he exercised through his earthly agents, witches.

In comparison to the rest of British America, Puritan New England had an unusually high number of witchcraft trials between the Pilgrims' arrival in 1620 and the outbreak of the Salem witch hysteria, just over seven decades later. Nonetheless, the vast majority of the trials did not end in a guilty verdict, and just 14 persons were hanged as witches in New England before 1692, with the first execution occurring in the colony of Connecticut in 1647. New England's record for convicting and executing witches would change dramatically during the Salem witchcraft panic of 1692–1693. Examining the general economic, political, and social environment of Salem and Massachusetts during the late seventeenth century provides important clues as to why colonial authorities were far more willing to convict—and execute—accused witches during this period than ever before in the history of New England.

On the Eve
of the Salem
Witchcraft Crisis

Over the centuries, historians have tried to better understand the unprecedented scale and intensity of the Salem witch hunt and trials in New England history by examining the particular political, economic, and social climate in which they took place. During the decade leading up to the witchcraft crisis of 1692–1693, the people of Massachusetts came under heavy stress from a number of sources. Uncertainty and fear gripped many of the colony's Puritan inhabitants, especially in the already conflict-ridden community of Salem, creating an environment in which traditional concerns regarding the threat of witchcraft developed into a full-fledged panic.

MASSACHUSETTS'S UNCERTAIN POLITICAL SITUATION

When the Salem witchcraft craze erupted in early 1692, political upheaval and uncertainty had plagued the Massachusetts colony for nearly eight years. At the root of the chaos was the loss of the colony's charter (fundamental laws) in 1684. Granted by the English king, Charles I, in 1629, the charter allowed the Puritan settlers an unusual degree of political and judicial independence, including the right to choose their own governor. Massachusetts's devoutly Puritan leadership restricted membership in the General Court, the colony's highest legislative and judicial body, and voting privileges to full members of the Puritan (Congregational) Church. This ensured that Puritans would remain the dominant political and religious force in Massachusetts, even if the colony's small number of non-Puritan English inhabitants eventually increased.

In 1649, the people of Massachusetts rejoiced when Puritan rebels won control of the English government, abolished the monarchy, and executed their longtime persecutor, King Charles I. Eleven years later, the colonists received the devastating news that the British monarchy had been restored under Charles II, the leaders of the Puritan revolution executed or imprisoned, and Anglicanism reestablished as England's state religion. During the two decades following the Restoration, growing numbers of Anglican merchants began migrating to Massachusetts's leading seaport, Boston. The merchants resented their exclusion from voting and holding political office and lobbied Charles II to overhaul Massachusetts's political system. To the dismay of the colony's Puritan majority, Charles gave in to the merchants' wishes and revoked Massachusetts Bay's original charter in 1684. Soon after, Charles's autocratic successor, James II, dissolved the Massachusetts General Court and the other New England colonies' chief legislative and judicial bodies and created a single "Dominion of New England," overseen by a royally appointed governor headquartered in Boston. The Dominion's arrogant royal governor, Sir Edmund Andros, outraged Massachusetts Puritans by founding New England's first Anglican Church— King's Chapel—in Boston; limiting New England towns to just one town meeting per year; and placing local militias under his direct control.

King James's numerous political opponents in Parliament, England's national legislative assembly, deposed the unpopular monarch in a virtually bloodless coup in 1688. Early the following year, Parliament had William and Mary of Orange installed as England's new king and queen. When word of the so-called Glorious Revolution in England reached Boston, the colonists lost no time in overthrowing James's despised appointee, Governor Andros. Yet, despite their relief at being rid of the tyrannical Andros, they were deeply anxious regarding Massachusetts's political and religious future. Technically, Massachusetts's original charter remained null and void, and no one knew what type of government England's new king and queen planned to impose on the colony. Troubling questions also arose regarding the status of the state-supported Anglican Church in the once exclusively Puritan colony and the colony's traditional, Old Testament–based legal code. Without a charter, even the title to the land the colonists lived on and farmed appeared in doubt.

THE MILITARY FRONT

At the same time that the people of Massachusetts were fretting about their political future, they were also becoming more and more worried about their Native American neighbors in New England and across the border in French-controlled Canada. Shortly after assuming power, William and Mary started a war with France that quickly spread to the two countries' North American colonies, where it was known as King William's War. The new conflict brought terror to northern Massachusetts when the French sent their Native American allies, the Abenaki, to attack English colonists in Maine, then part of the colony. Entire towns were burned to the ground, and hundreds of men, women, and children were massacred or taken captive during

A Puritan family in Deerfield, Massachusetts, barricades their house against an Indian raid. Puritans tended to view any threat to their New World mission, including from Native Americans, as inspired by Satan.

a string of Abenaki raids on frontier settlements in Maine and nearby New Hampshire.

In response to the escalating violence, the Massachusetts General Court sent a force of 2,000 soldiers to Quebec under Sir William Phips in the autumn of 1690 to capture New France's capital and hopefully bring the war to an end. Beset by bad weather and inadequate supplies, the Massachusetts expedition was a humiliating and expensive failure. Phips's battered fleet was forced to retreat to Boston in late October without having struck an effective blow against the enemy. In the wake of the disastrous expedition, Massachusetts was left with a huge debt and the disheartening prospect of continued Abenaki raids in its Maine territories. By this time, too, many people had become concerned that the bloody attacks would move southward into Essex County, which stretches along the Massachusetts coast from the New Hampshire border to a few miles north of Boston, and includes Salem. Reports of battles and raids in Maine and New Hampshire—including stories of gruesome tortures and murders—made their way into Essex County on a regular basis, some brought by local militiamen who had fought up there, others by refugees pushed southward by the violence. Rumors that Abenaki warriors had been spotted in the vicinity spread through many Essex communities, including Salem, which took in more than its share of war refugees. "The cumulative result" of these horrific stories and rumors, contends John Demos, was "nothing less than an overwhelming and highly toxic climate of fear."[1]

The colonists' fear of their Abenaki neighbors was firmly grounded in the "earthly dangers the Native Americans presented of sudden attack, arson, and massacre," writes historian Frances Hill. Yet, it also reflected a widely held belief that Native Americans posed a supernaturally based threat to the Puritan community. New England Puritans generally assumed that Indians were "agents of the Devil if not devils themselves," Hill notes.[2] According to the leading Boston clergyman and author, Cotton Mather, Native Americans were "well known to be horrid sorcerers and hellish conjurors and such as conversed with demons."[3] Puritan New Englanders were convinced that God had sent them to the American wilderness to build a pure Christian community—"a city upon a hill" for their mother country and the rest of Europe to emulate. Consequently, they tended to see any threat to their New World mission, including from Native Americans, as a Satan-inspired attack on God Himself.

FACTIONALISM IN SALEM VILLAGE

In Salem, the sense of crisis that enveloped Massachusetts in the wake of the loss of the colony's charter and the outbreak of King William's War was intensified by long-simmering local conflicts. During the late seventeenth century, Salem consisted of prosperous and commercialized Salem Town, the Essex County seat and most important New England seaport after Boston, and Salem Village (now Danvers), a chiefly agricultural community located six miles (9.6 kilometers) west of the town center. With a population of approximately 550 persons, Salem Village had a little more than a third as many residents as Salem Town in 1692. Salem Village, where the witchcraft craze originated in January of that year and where most of the accusers and many of the accused in the infamous trials resided, was an unusually factious, or divided, community. This factionalism appears to have had many roots. The bitterest division in Salem Village, however, was between traditional farming families with few or no economic ties to Salem Town, and those more forward-looking villagers who were abandoning small-scale farming for new commercial opportunities linked to the seaport.

Not surprisingly, the villagers taking advantage of the economic opportunities provided by Salem Town typically resided closer to the port in the eastern half of Salem Village, whereas the traditional, small-scale farmers typically resided farther from the port, in the village's western half. The incomes of the eastern, more commercially oriented villagers generally rose during the last several decades of the seventeenth century, while the incomes of the western farmers stagnated or declined. Many of these cash-strapped small farmers became disgruntled with living under the political control of larger Salem Town, whose leaders, they believed, had little appreciation for their more traditional economic concerns and values. They wanted Salem Village to break off from Salem Town and form its own independent community. Many of their neighbors in the eastern half of the village—including tradesmen, market-oriented farmers, and others with close economic ties to the seaport—strongly opposed the westerners' separatist campaign, however. Viewing their fortunes as dependent on the bustling seaport, they preferred to keep the village and town joined.

The two factions—the western farming families and the more business-minded eastern families—engaged in a bitter contest for control of the village and its future during the years leading up to the witchcraft craze. Countless disputes developed over property boundaries, taxation issues, and inheritances. Above all, the ongoing power struggle centered on the village's one independent institution: its Puritan church. Easterners, led by the Porter family, clashed with western farmers, led by the Putnam family, over whether to retain or dismiss a succession of ministers. During the 1680s, three preachers—James Bayley, George Burroughs, and Deodat Lawson—resigned from the church in frustration over the incessant quarreling among the congregation. One disgusted observer complained that "brother is against brother, and neighbors [are] against neighbors, all quarreling and smiting [abusing] one another."[4] A few years later, arbitrators called in from Salem Town to settle a heated dispute involving the Reverend Lawson cautioned the feuding villagers that "uncharitable expressions and uncomely reflections tossed to and fro . . . have a tendency to make such a gap as we fear, if not timely prevented, will let out peace and order and let in confusion and every evil work."[5]

SAMUEL PARRIS

Despite the arbitrators' warning, soon after Samuel Parris was hired to replace Lawson as pastor of the Salem Village church in 1689, the old bickering between the parish's traditionalist farmers and more entrepreneurial counterparts flared again. For the most part, the traditionalists backed Parris, while their more commercially oriented neighbors quickly emerged as the new pastor's harshest critics.

Parris, who was destined to play a central role in the development of the Salem witchcraft crisis, had no previous experience as a minister when he assumed the pulpit of the village's

Samuel Parris, minister of Salem Village, began to stir up his congregation when he preached of a devilish conspiracy against God's people. Conditions in the village were ripe for an outbreak of mass hysteria.

sole church in late 1689. He had been born into a middle-class Puritan family in London 36 years earlier. During his child-hood, his family moved to the British colony of Barbados in the eastern Caribbean, where his father became a prosperous sugar planter and merchant. Parris attended Harvard College in Cambridge, Massachusetts, for several years during his late teens, then returned to Barbados to work in the family business. In 1680, after a hurricane seriously damaged the family sugar plantation, Parris left the island for good to try his luck as a merchant in Boston. After eight years of only limited success, in 1688 Parris decided to make a major career change, abandoning business for the ministry. The next year, following lengthy negotiations with church representatives regarding his annual salary and firewood allotment, Parris accepted a position as Salem Village's new minister.

Parris's troubles with the feuding Salem congregation began within a year of his arrival in the village. Parris worried about his ability to provide for his family on his meager minister's salary, particularly after learning that several of his predecessors had been unable to collect their full pay from the parish. Consequently, he pushed his congregation to grant him full ownership of the parsonage (the official residence of a church's pastor). According to Larry Gragg, Parris finally got his wish in the autumn of 1690. Eager for allies in their efforts to separate Salem Village from Salem Town, the Putnam family threw their considerable influence behind his campaign to obtain permanent possession of the parsonage.[6] Parris's victory in the parsonage controversy, however, came at a heavy price for the new minister. The budding alliance between their pastor and the separatists angered the Porters and other villagers with close economic ties to Salem Town, and they began plotting to drive him from his pulpit.

A DEVILISH CONSPIRACY

After he finally secured title to the parsonage with the Putnams' assistance, Parris found himself under increasing attack by the Porter-led faction. In the midst of an ever-louder chorus of complaints about his character and qualifications, Parris went on the offensive. Without naming anyone directly, he began preaching about the growing "subversion" of the congregation by "shadowy forces of evil." His allegations of a Satan-inspired conspiracy against God's true followers in Salem became more urgent during the final month of 1691, after he learned that the village rate committee, which was controlled by the Porters, had voted against levying a tax to cover his salary for the coming year. Because "'rotten-hearted' people infiltrate even

THE BEWITCHMENT OF THE GOODWINS

When Cotton Mather's *Memorable Providences* was published in 1689—like his father Increase's book on the supernatural, *Illustrious Providences*—it quickly became a best seller in the greater Boston area, including Salem, just 16 miles (25.7 km) north of the capital. Regarding *Memorable Providences*, Frances Hill writes: "Cotton Mather spent his life trying to emulate his famous father. It is therefore hardly surprising that this, one of his earliest books, treats the same type of material . . . as the *Illustrious Providences*." But "Cotton's hysterical tone" in the book, notes Hill, was "very much his own."

The following passage from *Memorable Providences* focuses on the Goodwin bewitchment case that occurred in Boston just four years before the Salem trials. In the passage, Mather details what he calls the "direful effects of a . . . stupendous witchcraft" on stonemason John Goodwin's children, aged 5 to 13 years. Witches were believed to be capable of "possessing" their victims, causing them to suffer from convulsive fits and a variety of other terrifying symptoms. During their alleged bewitchment, the children were "tortured everywhere in a manner so very grievous, that it would have broke an heart of stone to have seen their agonies," wrote Mather:

innocent communities," Parris cautioned his flock, "surface appearances, superficial evidences of goodwill—none of these can be taken at face value."[7]

Parris's warnings of a devilish conspiracy against God's people hit home with many of his listeners in the wake of Massachusetts's recent political and military troubles and the increasingly acrimonious, or bitter, power struggle within Salem Village itself. His regular references in his sermons to

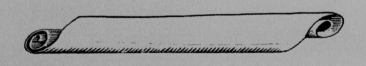

Sect. V. The variety of their tortures increased continually; and though about nine or ten at night they always had a release from their miseries, and ate and slept all night for the most part indifferently well, yet in the day time they were handled with so many sorts of ails, that it would require of us almost as much time to relate them all, as it did of them to endure them. Sometimes they would be deaf, sometimes dumb, and sometimes blind, and often, all this at once. One time their tongues would be drawn down their throats; another time they would be pulled out upon their chins, to a prodigious length. . . . . They would make most piteous outcries, that they were cut with knives, and struck with blows that they could not bear. Their necks would be broken, so that their neck-bone would seem dissolved unto them that felt after it; and yet on the sudden, it would become, again so stiff that there was no stirring of their heads; . . . . Thus they lay some weeks most pitiful spectacles; and this while as a further demonstration of witchcraft in these horrid effects, when I went to prayer by one of them, that was very desirous to hear what I said, the child utterly lost her hearing till our prayer was over.

* All quotations are from Frances Hill, *The Salem Witchcraft Trials Reader.* New York: Da Capo Press, 2000, pp. 17–19.

witches as especially powerful members of Satan's earthly army also must have struck a responsive chord with many members of his congregation. For the most part, Europe's interest in hunting and prosecuting suspected witches had been declining steadily since the mid-seventeenth century. Thanks in large measure to the publication of popular books on the subject by two of the colony's most respected ministers and scholars, however, interest in diabolical witchcraft was stronger than ever in Massachusetts during the years leading up to the Salem witchcraft crisis.

During the 1680s, Increase and Cotton Mather, New England's most celebrated father-and-son clerics, wrote best-selling books on witchcraft's evil power. Both Mathers were concerned that Europeans were becoming complacent about the dangers of witchcraft and wanted to ensure that New Englanders did not make the same mistake. With that in mind, Increase devoted several long chapters in his *An Essay for the Recording of Illustrious Providences* to witchcraft scares in Puritan New England since its founding five decades earlier. Among the sensational cases he covered in his book, which underwent three separate printings between 1684 and 1689, was that of Elizabeth Knapp, a 16-year-old maidservant from Groton, Massachusetts. For several months in 1671 and 1672, she suffered from mysterious fits, "sometimes weeping, sometimes laughing, sometimes roaring hideously, with violent motions and agitations of her body," Mather reported.[8] After Knapp confessed to dabbling in witchcraft and tearfully repented of her sin, Mather noted, the teenager's fits suddenly ended, never to return.

Five years after his father's book appeared, Cotton Mather published an even more comprehensive chronicle of witchcraft in New England, entitled *Memorable Providences, Relating to Witchcrafts and Possessions*. Like Increase's work, *Memorable Providences* was a best seller, going through several Boston editions within just a few years. In his book, Cotton paid particular attention to a case of alleged bewitchment in which he was personally involved. In the summer of 1688, four young children of Bostonian John Goodwin began suffering from bizarre fits. When physicians failed to find anything medically wrong with the two girls and two boys, the terrified parents sought the assistance of several Boston ministers, including Cotton Mather. Like his father, Cotton was a firm believer in the power of the supernatural, and he soon became convinced that the Goodwins were victims of witchcraft. Eventually, Goody (short for "Goodwife") Glover, an impoverished washerwoman who had recently argued with the Goodwins over some missing property, was convicted of bewitching the children and sentenced to hang. Mather's lurid description of the children's sufferings in his book, combined with the fact that Glover's execution marked the first time a suspected witch had been hanged in New England in more than 20 years, brought the case enormous notoriety.

Historians cannot say with certainty whether Samuel Parris or anyone else in Salem Village owned Cotton or Increase Mather's books on what both ministers clearly considered as the grave threat posed by diabolical witchcraft to the Puritan community. It seems probable, however, that Parris and many of his parishioners were familiar with the Mathers' popular exposés of demonic possession in nearby Boston and elsewhere in New England. And in early 1692, the Mathers' supposedly factual accounts of witches and demons would have primed the villagers to listen to the extraordinary accusations of the two young Salem girls who launched what was to become the deadliest witch hunt in American history.

The Accusations Begin

In the atmosphere of anxiety and contentiousness that pervaded Salem Village by the beginning of 1692, two young girls in the household of Reverend Samuel Parris—his 9-year-old daughter, Betty, and 11-year-old niece, Abigail Williams—started suffering strange and frightening "fits" and "distempers [mental disturbances]."[1] For months, Parris had been warning his congregation about a shadowy, Satan-inspired conspiracy against God's people. Now it seemed that the evil conspiracy had openly erupted, and in the minister's own home.

BETTY AND ABIGAIL'S "CRUEL SUFFERINGS"

Betty and Abigail's disturbing symptoms first developed soon after they secretly experimented with fortune-telling sometime in January 1692. According to a contemporary account by John Hale, a minister from the nearby town of Beverly, one day when the girls had been left unsupervised in the parsonage, they decided to devise a sort of primitive crystal ball using egg whites dropped into a bowl of water. Supposedly, they believed their future husbands' occupations would be revealed by the shape that the egg white formed in the water. To the girls' horror, the floating egg white appeared to take on the outline of a coffin. Since the Puritan clergy frowned upon fortune-telling, warning that all types of magic were dangerous invitations to the forces of evil, the girls would have had reason to feel anxious and guilty already about their clandestine experiment. "The coffin," writes author Gail Collins, "probably made them feel they were looking into the face of their own doom."[2]

Shortly after the coffin episode, Betty and Abigail started to suffer severe physical and mental anguish—or to fake such anguish—it is impossible to know which. According to John Hale, the girls

> were bitten and pinched by invisible agents; their arms, necks, and backs turned this way and that way, and returned back again, so as it was impossible for them to do of themselves, and beyond the power of any epileptic fits, or natural disease to effect. Sometimes they were taken dumb, their mouths stopped, their throats choked, their limbs wracked and tormented so as might move an heart of stone, to sympathize with them. . . . I will not enlarge in the description of their cruel sufferings, because they were in all things afflicted as bad as John Goodwins' children at Boston, in the year 1688.[3]

Hale was not the only contemporary observer to notice the similarities between Betty and Abigail's bizarre afflictions and the sufferings of the Goodwin children four years earlier. The story of the Goodwins' possession was widely known in eastern Massachusetts through Cotton Mather's account

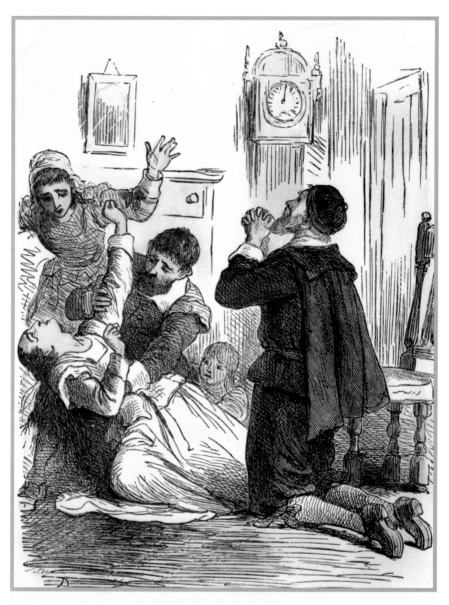

Puritan minister Cotton Mather uses prayer to attempt to save a soul from witchcraft.

of the episode in his best seller, *Memorable Providences*, "as well as through word of mouth," observes historian Bernard Rosenthal.[4] Writing nearly a century after the infamous Salem trials, the Massachusetts historian and witchcraft skeptic Thomas Hutchinson contended that "the conformity between the behavior of Goodwin's children and most of the supposed bewitched at Salem . . . is so exact, as to leave no room to doubt the stories had been read by the [afflicted] persons themselves, or had been told to them by others who had read them." However, Hutchinson remarked, "this conformity, instead of giving suspicion," as he believed it should have, "was urged in confirmation of the truth of both."[5]

A SHOCKING DIAGNOSIS

As Hutchinson noted in his account of the episode, Betty and Abigail's singular behavior, which was so reminiscent of the Goodwins' behavior after their neighbor allegedly bewitched the children, was taken very seriously by the village community. Deeply unsettled by the girls' puzzling fits, Parris asked a local physician, William Griggs, to examine them. Griggs could find nothing medically wrong with the minister's daughter and niece. But instead of suggesting they might be suffering from hysteria (a feature of certain mental disorders in which a patient experiences physical symptoms that have a psychological, rather than a physiological, basis) or merely playacting, the doctor jumped to the most terrifying possible conclusion. Diabolical witchcraft, or "the evil hand," was the most likely cause of Betty and Abigail's suffering, Griggs declared.[6] Parris, a firm believer in the destructive power of witchcraft, never seems to have questioned the doctor's extraordinary diagnosis. After several weeks of fasting and intense prayer failed to have any effect on the girls' condition, Parris asked several ministers from Salem Town and other nearby communities to meet with Betty and Abigail. Like Dr. Griggs, the ministers discerned "the hand of Satan" in the girls' afflictions. Nonetheless, they urged Parris to be patient and refrain from taking hasty action. "Sit still and wait upon the Providence [divine guidance] of God," the clerics advised.[7]

As word began to spread through Salem that someone had been using witchcraft to torment the minister's daughter and niece, many villagers became alarmed. Their apprehensions grew when several other residents of Salem Village began to show signs of supernatural possession. By late February, two friends and neighbors of Betty and Abigail were also acting bewitched. They were 12-year-old Ann Putnam, the daughter of Thomas Putnam, and 17-year-old Elizabeth Hubbard, the orphaned great-niece and servant of Dr. Griggs. The "afflicted girls," as they came to be known, quickly acquired the status of local celebrities as their fellow villagers and ministers from neighboring towns flocked to their homes to pray with them or simply gawk at their strange fits.[8] Being the center of attention was an unusual—and undoubtedly exhilarating—experience for the four girls. "As daughters and servants who occupied the lower ranks of household hierarchies, their normal role was to be seen and not heard, to tend to others' needs, and to acquiesce in all tasks required of them," observes historian Mary Beth Norton.[9] According to author Gail Collins:

Adolescent girls were the least powerful people in a New England community. Their education was usually limited to learning enough to read the Bible. Many of them, even those from well-to-do families, were sent away from home to work as servants, to learn domestic skills and the proper spirit of obedience. . . . But suddenly, important adults were trooping to their homes to see them and talk with them. Everything they said was taken seriously.[10]

Parris's clerical advisers had counseled prayer combined with a cautious wait-and-see approach in the face of Salem Village's growing witchcraft problem. But "not everybody was content with such a passive response," write Boyer and Nissenbaum.[11] According to traditional English folk magic, witches might be detected in a number of ways, including by baking a "witch cake" made with the urine of her victims. Although Puritan ministers forbade their flocks from dabbling in magic of any kind, a concerned villager named Mary Sibley decided something had to be done to end the girls' suffering. One day when Reverend Parris was away from home, Sibley convinced his two West Indian slaves, Tituba and John Indian, to make a witch cake from rye meal mixed with Betty and Abigail's urine, and then feed the concoction to the family dog. Historian Marilynne Roach explains the reasoning behind Sibley's clandestine experiment: "If someone sent evil pain" to Betty and Abigail, writes Roach, "part of that person was in the evil that afflicted them, the sufferers. By tormenting the tormented substance—in this case their urine, now safely away from their bodies—it was hoped to injure the essence of the evil-doer still lurking within it. Baking the cake and letting the dog devour it was an attempt to hurt the responsible witch, who might then reveal herself."[12]

THE FIRST ACCUSATIONS

Despite Sibley's efforts to keep the witch cake a secret, Parris found out about it. He scolded her from his pulpit, reminding his congregation that any attempt to practice magic was sinful and could unleash "diabolical" supernatural forces in the community.[13] Around the same time, Betty and Abigail's symptoms worsened, and they began claiming that they could see the shapes of actual people who tortured them. Prodded by Parris to identify their tormentors, the girls named Tituba, alleging that her specter—or spirit form—had bit, pinched, and throttled them, even though no one else could see the attacks. When Parris confronted his slave regarding the accusations, Tituba denied being a witch, stubbornly maintaining her innocence even after Ann Putnam and Elizabeth Hubbard also claimed that her specter had assaulted them. Within days of denouncing Tituba as a witch, all four of the "afflicted girls" had identified two additional villagers, Sarah Good and Sarah Osborne, as their tormenters.

It seems likely that few of their fellow villagers were surprised when Tituba, Good, and Osborne were named as the first suspects in the community's burgeoning witchcraft crisis. All three fit the usual profile of witch-hunt victims in New England. Like nearly 80 percent of accused witches in New England, they were female. The reasons for the predominance of women among New England witch suspects, writes John Demos, "certainly included the same female-inferiority principle that held throughout the early modern English and European world, where women were seen as inherently 'weak,' especially from a moral standpoint, and thus liable to 'seduction' by the Devil."[14] Also in common with the typical New England—and European—witch suspect, the three women were either of low socioeconomic standing or had somehow violated social norms. Tituba was a slave, probably of Arawak Indian heritage, who had been brought to Massachusetts from Barbados by Samuel Parris. Sarah Good was an ill-tempered beggar who reportedly cursed her neighbors when they refused to give her food or money. Sarah Osborne was a sickly middle-aged housewife with a scandalous past. Rumor had it that after the death of her first husband, she had lived in sin for years with her Irish farmhand, Alexander Osborne, before the couple finally married.

On February 29, 1692, probably after consulting with Samuel Parris, four of the village church's most prominent male members, including Ann's father and uncle, decided to take action against the accused witches. That day they filed formal complaints against Tituba, Good, and Osborne with Salem Town magistrates Jonathan Corwin and John Hathorne. Hathorne and Corwin ordered that the three suspects be arrested and taken to Nathaniel Ingersoll's tavern in Salem Village for questioning. They also instructed the four afflicted girls and "any other person

Samuel Parris's slave Tituba warns some of Salem's children about witches in this illustration. Tituba was accused by the afflicted girls of being a witch.

or persons that can give evidence" to report to Ingersoll's establishment the following morning.[15]

THE TWO SARAHS ARE INTERROGATED

By 10:00 A.M. on March 1, when the questioning of the three accused witches was scheduled to begin, so many curious villagers had gathered at Ingersoll's tavern that the examinations had to be moved to the nearby meetinghouse (church). Sarah Good was the first of the defendants to be interrogated by Hathorne and Corwin. The tone of their questioning was accusatory from the start, as clerk Ezekiel Cheever's record of the March 1 proceedings in Salem Village plainly reveals.

Magistrate Hathorne opened the examination by bluntly demanding, "Sarah Good, what evil spirit have you familiarity with?" When Good replied, "None," Hathorne pointed at her four accusers, Ann Putnam, Betty Parris, Abigail Williams, and Elizabeth Hubbard and asked, "Why do you hurt these children?" Although Good adamantly denied hurting the girls, Hathorne immediately followed up with yet another leading question. "Who do you employ then to do it?" he demanded. "I employ nobody," she insisted. "I am falsely accused."[16]

Hathorne next ordered Ann, Betty, Abigail, and Elizabeth to look directly at Good to confirm whether she was one of their tormentors. After making eye contact with Sarah, the girls immediately fell into terrifying fits, writhing and shrieking in apparent agony. When they had sufficiently recovered their composure to testify, all four "positively accused her of hurting them sundry [many] times," Cheever noted.[17] After Good again denied harming the girls, they became "all dreadfully tortured and tormented," according to a contemporary account, and screamed that Sarah's specter was lunging at them.[18] When the magistrates continued to press Good regarding her role in the girls' afflictions, desperate to save herself, Good blurted out that it was Sarah Osborne who hurt the children, not her.

Good's plight went from bad to worse when a village couple who had allowed her to live in their home for a time testified that Sarah was so irritable and spiteful that they had finally turned her out. During the two years after Good was forced from their house, the couple reported, 17 of their cattle had died mysteriously, leading them to wonder whether she had bewitched the animals. To add insult to injury, Sarah's own husband, William Good, who had recently served a stint in jail

When Betty, Abigail, Ann, and Elizabeth made eye contact with Sarah Good at her trial, they fell into fits, effectively condemning her. This illustration shows an accused witch facing Salem's afflicted girls in court.

for failing to pay his debts, turned on her. Sarah had been a terrible wife to him, William testified, and her combative personality had persuaded him she was "an enemy to all good."[19] The night before the hearing, William had even made a special visit to the village constable to inform him of an oddly shaped blemish he had noticed below his wife's right shoulder. The blemish, William helpfully pointed out, might be a "witch's mark," a sign that Sarah had made a secret pact to serve Satan.

The second Sarah to be accused of witchcraft in Salem Village fared little better in her examination than the first. Following the same accusatory pattern of questioning with Osborne as they had with Good, the magistrates demanded to know "what evil spirit" she had "familiarity with" and why she "hurt" the four girls.[20] "In short, guilt was assumed; the aim was simply to obtain confirmation," writes John Demos.[21] Once again, Hathorne ordered Betty, Abigail, Ann, and Elizabeth to make eye contact with the suspect, leading to a new bout of noisy fits in the afflicted girls.

In contrast to the destitute Good, Osborne was solidly middle class, but her standing in the village community was hardly better. Aside from the rumors that she had cohabited with her husband before they married, many of Osborne's fellow villagers also disapproved of her spotty church attendance record. When pressed by the magistrates regarding her year-long absence from Sunday services, Osborne blamed her poor health, an argument that her interrogators failed to find convincing, even though her husband, Alexander, testified Sarah had been too weak to leave their house for months.

TITUBA'S SHOCKING CONFESSION

The last of the three witch suspects to be interrogated on March 1 was Samuel Parris's West Indian slave, Tituba. As soon as Tituba entered the meetinghouse, the girls suffered even more violent fits than they had during Good and Osborne's examinations. At the beginning of the interrogation, Tituba strongly denied practicing witchcraft or hurting the girls. But she soon changed her story under the magistrates' relentless and hostile questioning. "Step by step," writes Demos, Tituba "was threatened and coaxed . . . into an astonishing set of confessions."[22] By testifying that Sarah Osborne had hurt the afflicted girls, Sarah Good had already bolstered the credibility of the young accusers. Tituba went considerably farther than Good had in her testimony, offering vivid accounts of how she had been coerced into serving Satan and of her many encounters with other witches and their familiar spirits. A familiar spirit was an animal-shaped specter given to a witch by the devil; they were said to feed on the blood of their witch masters. In lurid detail, Tituba described being visited by the specter of a mysterious, black-garbed man who threatened to kill her unless she obeyed him; fighting off ghostly cats who tried to "thrust" her "into the fire"; and flying through the sky on a wooden pole to huge witch gatherings.[23] (Although the broomstick had been portrayed as a popular mode of travel for witches since the Middle Ages, broom riding was not mentioned in any of the Salem records.) Tituba also confessed to having pinched the afflicted children, but only under pressure from Satan and her fellow witches, and claimed to have witnessed the specters of Osborne, Good, and several other unnamed witches hurt the girls on many occasions.

By the time she had finished her startling testimony, Tituba had persuaded many in her audience of the guilt of Good and Osborne and the fundamental truthfulness of the young accusers. She had also raised fears regarding a broader witchcraft conspiracy with her references to unnamed accomplices, including the large numbers at the witch meetings that she supposedly attended. The same night of Tituba's examination, two local farmers, William Allen and John Hughes, reported seeing a strange beast crouched on the road ahead of them as they were returning home from the meetinghouse. When the men approached the beast, it suddenly assumed the shape of three women. Although the women vanished into the darkness almost as abruptly as they had appeared, Allen and Hughes were certain that they had glimpsed Tituba, Osborne, and Good—or rather their specters—since all three defendants had been placed under heavy guard immediately following their examinations.

In the wake of the March 1 hearing, and particularly Tituba's unsettling testimony, many Salem villagers had become convinced that their community was in a state of siege. Even with Tituba, Osborne, and Good locked away in prison, people were

THE QUESTIONING OF TITUBA

Historians can only speculate regarding Tituba's motives in confessing to witchery. Many believe that her fantastical confession was an attempt to protect herself from further punishment by telling her interrogators what she thought they wanted to hear. In her confession, she apologized for any pain she had caused the girls and emphasized that she had been compelled to sign the devil's book under threat of death. In the following excerpts from the written record of Tituba's examination by Magistrate John Hathorne, on March 1, 1692, "H" stands for Hathorne and "T" for Tituba.

  (H) Did you never see the Devil.

  (T) The devil came to me and bid me serve him.

  (H) Who have you seen.

  (T) Four women sometimes hurt the children.

  (H) Who were they.

  (T) Goode [Goody] Osburn and Sarah Good and I do not know
      who the others were. . . .

deeply uneasy. Adding to their apprehensions, the strange fits of the afflicted continued unabated, and new "victims" joined the original group of bewitched girls. Among them were 17-year-old Mercy Lewis, a servant in Ann Putnam's house; Ann's cousin, 17-year-old Mary Walcott; 20-year-old Mary Warren; 18-year-old Susannah Sheldon; and two older married women—Ann's mother, Ann Putnam Sr., and Sarah Bibber.

The list of the accused grew right along with the victim group and, by the end of March, it had come to include a

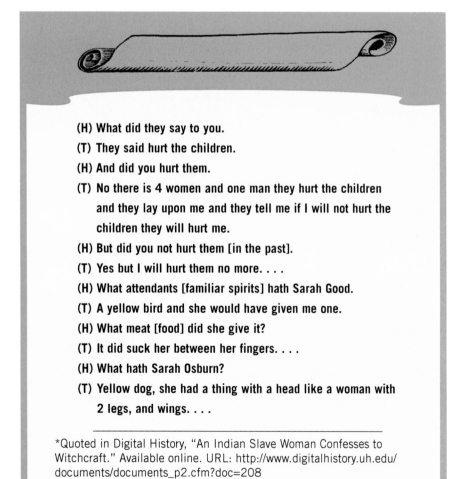

(H) What did they say to you.

(T) They said hurt the children.

(H) And did you hurt them.

(T) No there is 4 women and one man they hurt the children and they lay upon me and they tell me if I will not hurt the children they will hurt me.

(H) But did you not hurt them [in the past].

(T) Yes but I will hurt them no more. . . .

(H) What attendants [familiar spirits] hath Sarah Good.

(T) A yellow bird and she would have given me one.

(H) What meat [food] did she give it?

(T) It did suck her between her fingers. . . .

(H) What hath Sarah Osburn?

(T) Yellow dog, she had a thing with a head like a woman with 2 legs, and wings. . . .

*Quoted in Digital History, "An Indian Slave Woman Confesses to Witchcraft." Available online. URL: http://www.digitalhistory.uh.edu/documents/documents_p2.cfm?doc=208

four-year-old child, Sarah Good's daughter Dorcas, and several respectable village matrons: Martha Corey, Elizabeth Proctor, Rebecca Nurse, and Sarah Cloyce. Their arrests signaled a major shift in Salem's budding witchcraft crisis. The typical New England witch outbreak resulted in just one or two people, usually social misfits, being accused. In Salem Village, eight persons—including the wife of a prosperous local innkeeper (Proctor); a devout churchgoer (Corey); and a widely beloved matriarch (Nurse) and her pious, farmwife sister (Cloyce)—had been arrested on charges of witchcraft within a matter of weeks. But their shocking arrests were only the beginning. No one could have imagined in late March 1692 that by the end of the spring, nearly 100 persons would have been detained in Salem and nearby communities on suspicion of diabolical witchcraft.

The First Trials

By April 1692, Salem's witch accusers had broadened their attacks beyond the usual female outcasts targeted in most New England witch hunts to include several respectable villagers. The first to be arrested was Martha Corey, an outspoken, middle-aged farmwife and longtime church member. Ann Putnam and the other afflicted girls accused Corey after Martha made it known around the village that she considered the witchcraft scare utter nonsense. When Magistrates Hathorne and Corwin questioned Corey in the meetinghouse, the afflicted girls thrashed and wailed. One village woman who had come to watch the proceedings was so upset by the girls' frightening symptoms that she hurled her shoe at Corey, hitting her in the head. Instead of supporting his parishioner, Samuel Parris contributed to the hostile, even paranoid, atmosphere surrounding Corey's examination by warning the rest of his congregation that even seemingly pious church members may be Satan's servants. "Christ knows how many devils [are] among us," he preached after Martha's arrest, "whether one or ten or 20. . . . The Devil hath been raised amongst us, and his rage is vehement and terrible."[1]

"WHAT SIN HATH GOD FOUND OUT IN ME?"

Rebecca Nurse, Sarah Cloyce, and Elizabeth Proctor, like their fellow villager Martha Corey, had reputations as upstanding community members and devout Puritans. Yet during the early spring of 1692, all three were arrested on suspicion of witchcraft and dragged off to the meetinghouse for questioning. Seventy-one years old and in frail health, Rebecca Nurse was stunned when a group of concerned friends warned her that several of the afflicted girls and Ann Putnam Sr. were claiming Nurse's specter had bitten and "almost choked" them.[2] "What sin hath God found out in me unrepented of, that He should lay such an affliction upon me in my old age?" Nurse wondered sadly.[3] At Nurse's packed hearing, her accusers shrieked so loudly when she denied ever hurting them that the entire courtroom was alarmed.

Soon after Nurse's arrest, her younger sister and loyal defender, Sarah Cloyce, was also imprisoned on suspicion of witchcraft. Two of Cloyce's chief accusers were members of Samuel Parris's household: Abigail Williams and Tituba's husband, John Indian. Parris's daughter Betty, however, had no part in Cloyce's arrest or hearing, despite her central role in helping to spark the witch hunt in January. By early April, when Cloyce's public examination took place, Betty's worried mother had sent the nine-year-old to live with relatives in Salem Town, and her name never again appeared on an arrest warrant. Only after the witchcraft crisis ended in late 1693 did Betty Parris return home to the village parsonage.

Soon after they accused Rebecca Nurse of witchcraft, Abigail Williams and John Indian also accused Elizabeth

Proctor of attacking them. At Elizabeth's hearing, the Salem witch hunt expanded to include its first male victim when Abigail and Ann testified that Elizabeth's husband, John, a well-off innkeeper and farmer who had publicly scoffed at the girls' claims of bewitchment, was tormenting them too. Several other villagers also testified against John and Elizabeth, including farmer Benjamin Gould, who claimed that the Proctors' specters, along with those of Sarah Cloyce and Rebecca Nurse, appeared in his bedchamber one night. After this terrifying encounter, Gould reported, he was left with such excruciating pain in his foot that he could not wear a shoe for a full two days afterward.

SPIRALING ACCUSATIONS

During the month of April, the pace of the witchcraft accusations quickened as dozens of new people came under suspicion. Most were residents of Salem Village, but several lived in Salem Town and smaller neighboring communities in Essex County. On April 11, Massachusetts authorities responded to the growing crisis by moving the witch examinations from Salem Village to more populous Salem Town, where the colony's deputy governor, Thomas Danforth; six magistrates; and throngs of spectators began attending the hearings. Danforth's involvement in the proceedings lent them a new seriousness, and the pace of witchcraft accusations in Salem and nearby communities such as Topsfield and Ipswich accelerated further.

By mid-May, more than 50 suspects were being held in jails in Salem Town and Boston. The majority of them were middle-aged women like Mary Eastey, the 58-year-old sister of Rebecca Nurse and Sarah Cloyce. But at least a dozen men, including several prominent residents or former residents of Salem Village and Salem Town, were also arrested. Among the suspects were two elderly and well-off inhabitants of Salem Village, George Jacobs and Martha Corey's husband, Giles; George Burroughs, a former pastor of the Salem Village

Conditions in the jails in which accused witches were held were abominable. This is the exterior of the Old Witch Jail and Dungeon in Salem.

church; and Philip English, one of Salem Town's leading merchants. English and his wife, Mary, who was arrested shortly before her husband, managed to escape to New York in August

1692—possibly by bribing their guards. As was true in most other New England witch hunts, a substantial portion of the males targeted in the Salem witchcraft panic, including Philip English, Giles Corey, and John Proctor, were married to women who had already been charged with witchcraft. Many others were blood relatives or friends of previously accused women.

"SUBURBS OF HELL"

"Because no single facility could begin to hold them all," observes Larry Gragg, authorities dispersed the growing number of accused in Salem and nearby communities to jails in Salem Town, Boston (where the colony's largest prison was located), and Ipswich.[4] Conditions in all the prisons were appalling. Massachusetts's dungeon-like jails, remarked one visitor to the colony just before the witchcraft outbreak, were little more than "suburbs of Hell."[5] The shoddily constructed buildings were stifling hot in the summer and frigidly cold in the winter. Not surprisingly, infectious diseases spread rapidly in the crowded and rat-infested jails. One of the first people to be arrested for witchcraft in Salem Village, Sarah Osborne, fell sick and died in Boston's jail in early May, and the infant child of Sarah Good also died there sometime during the spring of 1692. According to historian Frances Hill, witch suspects were not only deprived of adequate medical treatment but also subjected to regular physical and psychological abuse. "They were treated by wardens and visitors with deliberate cruelty, fair game for sadism since they were enemies of God and mankind," she asserts.[6]

Adding to their suffering, prisoners were chained to the walls of their cells to prevent their specters from escaping and tormenting innocent townspeople. Even Sarah Good's four-year-old daughter, Dorcas, was kept in heavy leg irons. Dorcas was carted off to jail soon after her mother's arrest. The little girl's chief accuser, Ann Putnam, claimed that Dorcas's specter had viciously bit and pinched her after Ann refused to sign the devil's book. Although she was never brought to trial, Dorcas would remain in jail for more than six months. Eighteen years after Dorcas's ordeal, William Good petitioned the Massachusetts General Court to pay for a caretaker for his 22-year-old daughter. Dorcas's imprisonment, he declared, had taken a permanent toll on her mental and physical health. "She was in prison seven or eight months and being chained in the dungeon was so hardly [cruelly] used and terrified that she hath ever since been very chargeable, having little or no reason to govern herself," he testified.[7] (By "very chargeable," Good meant that his daughter needed expensive, nearly constant care.)

A NEW CHARTER AND GOVERNOR

Growing numbers of witch suspects were being hauled off to jail in Salem, Boston, and nearby communities during the late winter and spring of 1692. Yet, as of mid-May, only preliminary witchcraft examinations had been held in Salem. Not a single trial had taken place. "Indeed, there *could* be none," observe Paul Boyer and Stephen Nissenbaum, "for during these months Massachusetts was in the touchy position of being without a legally established government."[8] In the absence of such a government, witchcraft trials and other types of capital court cases (death penalty cases) could not be heard in the colony.

Nearly a decade earlier, the Crown had revoked Massachusetts's original charter, which had given the colony an extraordinary degree of political and judicial independence, and placed all of New England under the authority of a tyrannical royal governor, Sir Edmund Andros. Five years later, following the overthrow of the unpopular King James II and the installation of William and Mary as England's new rulers, the people of Massachusetts toppled Andros in a virtually bloodless coup. Over the next two years, Puritan leaders tried unsuccessfully to persuade William and Mary to restore their original charter, even sending the prominent Boston minister and president of

Sir William Phips (*above*) became the first royal governor of Massachusetts. Immediately after his appointment, Phips began to deal with the witchcraft epidemic in Salem.

Harvard College, Increase Mather, to London to lobby the royal government on their behalf.

In early 1692, Mather sent word home that Massachusetts's long political limbo was about to end: The colony had been granted a new royal charter, and he would soon be returning to Boston with the document. The charter was not all that the colonists could have hoped for, to say the least. Most significantly, instead of allowing colonial legislators to choose their governor, as they had done under the old charter, the new charter made the governor a royal appointee. Nonetheless, "as a concession to Mather," writes historian Francis Bremer, "the Boston clergyman was allowed to name the first royal governor, with only one stipulation, that it be a military man."[9] Increase selected a member of his Boston church, Sir William Phips, the commander of Massachusetts's failed military assault on Quebec the previous autumn. On May 14, 1692, Mather and Phips, who had joined his pastor in London several months earlier, sailed into Boston Harbor with the new charter. Now that Massachusetts again had a legally constituted government, authorities could finally move forward with formal prosecution of the accused witches crowding the colony's prisons.

THE COURT OF OYER AND TERMINER

Upon disembarking in Boston, Governor Phips was immediately greeted with the disquieting news that a major witchcraft outbreak had erupted in Salem Village, and jails in Salem and Boston were overflowing with suspects. Convinced of the seriousness of the situation, Phips took immediate action. Within days of his arrival, he approved the creation of an emergency tribunal, the Court of Oyer and Terminer, to investigate and render a judgment on the huge backlog of witchcraft cases then pending in Salem. (*Oyer* and *terminer* are French words that mean "to hear" and "to determine," respectively.) To act as chief justice of the court, Phips appointed William Stoughton, Massachusetts's new lieutenant governor.

Phips's decree proclaiming the establishment of the Court of Oyer and Terminer on May 27, 1692, outlined his main reasons for creating the emergency tribunal. In addition to

Bridget Bishop was the first woman to be executed on charges of witchcraft in Salem. This illustration depicts her hanging.

Stoughton, the decree named eight men, all of them respected members of the Salem and Boston communities, to serve as judges in the Court of Oyer and Terminer:

> Upon consideration that there are many criminal offenders now in custody, some whereof have lain long, and many inconveniences attending the thronging of the jails

at this hot season of the year, there being no judicatories or courts of justice yet established: Ordered, that a Special Commission of Oyer and Terminer be made out to William Stoughton, John Richards, Nathaniel Saltonstall, Wait Winthrop, Bartholomew Gedney, Samuel Sewall, John Hathorne, Jonathan Corwin and Peter Sergeant, Esquires, assigning them to be justices, or any five of them.[10]

WILLIAM PHIPS AND WILLIAM STOUGHTON

After assuming office in 1692, Massachusetts's new governor, Sir William Phips, and lieutenant governor, William Stoughton, would play central roles in determining the path that Salem's witchcraft crisis followed. Although the two men came from very different backgrounds, both were firm believers in the malevolent power of witchcraft.

William Phips was born near the port town of Kennebec, Maine, on February 2, 1651. The twenty-sixth child of a gunsmith, Phips grew up in poverty and never had any formal schooling. Ambitious and adventurous, when he was still in his teens he decided to set off on foot for New England's chief seaport, Boston, nearly 200 miles (321.8 km) south of his hometown. Once there, Phips found employment on a merchant ship, quickly working his way up to the position of captain. In 1687, he led a successful sea expedition to recover treasure from a Spanish galleon that had sunk off the Bahamas several decades before. While most of the lucrative salvage went to the investors who funded the expedition and to the royal treasury, Phips was allowed to keep 16 percent of the booty and was knighted by King James II for his efforts.

Suddenly a man of wealth and prestige, Phips returned to Boston in 1688, where he became a leader in the colonial opposition to Edmund Andros. In May 1689, a few months after Andros's overthrow, Massachusetts officials asked Phips to lead a large force against the

Most of the nine magistrates had previous experience with witchcraft cases, and all but two—John Richards and Nathaniel Saltonstall—had observed one or more of the preliminary examinations conducted by Hathorne and Corwin. With the selection at the end of May of a jury of male residents, every one a church member in good standing, all was in place for the first actual trial of the Salem witchcraft crisis.

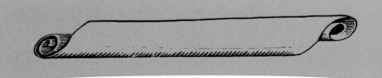

French garrison at Port Royal (in present-day Nova Scotia, Canada). Although Phips's second military expedition against New France, the siege of Quebec in October 1690, would prove disastrous, his Port Royal expedition was a rousing success and made Phips a hero back home in Massachusetts, paving the way for his appointment as royal governor three years later.

Lieutenant Governor William Stoughton, the man whom Phips selected to be chief justice of the Court of Oyer and Terminer, was born 20 years before the royal governor, on September 30, 1631. A native of England, Stoughton immigrated to Massachusetts with his parents as a young child. In contrast to Phips's impoverished family, the Stoughtons were large landowners capable of providing their children with the finest education money could buy. William earned a bachelor's degree from Harvard at age 19 and a master's degree from Oxford University in England 3 years later. Returning to Massachusetts, Stoughton served as a preacher in Dorchester's Puritan church for several years before entering political life as a selectman and member of the General Court, Massachusetts Bay's chief legislative and judicial body. Stoughton's extensive knowledge of both theology and the law made him a logical choice to head the new tribunal established by Phips in May 1692 to hear witchcraft cases.

THE FIRST TRIAL AND CONVICTION

On June 2, just one week after the Court of Oyer and Terminer was formally created, the special tribunal convened for the first time in Salem Town. Two days earlier, Thomas Newton, the special prosecutor for the trials, had ordered the return to Salem of seven suspects imprisoned in Boston, including Sarah Good; Rebecca Nurse; John and Elizabeth Proctor; and Bridget Bishop, a middle-aged housewife from Salem Town known for her hot temper. (Many chroniclers of the Salem witchcraft episode have mistakenly identified Bridget Bishop as a Salem tavern owner; she was actually the wife of a local sawyer, a person who saws wood for a living.) Bishop would have the distinction of being the first defendant tried by the new emergency tribunal. As it turned out, she would also be the first person to be convicted and executed in the Salem witchcraft craze. Unfortunately, the official records of the Court of Oyer and Terminer were lost long ago. Nonetheless, contemporary accounts, including those by Samuel Parris and Cotton Mather, have allowed historians to piece together important details of Bishop's trial and succeeding witchcraft trials in Salem.

Bishop's gender, age, combativeness, and personal eccentricities, particularly her flashy style of dress featuring "a red . . . bodice bordered and looped with different colors," all made her a typical witch-hunt target in Puritan New England.[11] In fact, rumors that Bishop was a witch had been circulating for decades in Salem and nearby communities. At her June 2 trial, nearly a dozen of Bishop's current and former neighbors testified against her, reporting that after quarreling with the defendant, their family members or livestock had suffered strange accidents or developed mysterious, sometimes fatal, ailments. Even more damaging, two laborers testified that, while repairing a cellar wall in Bishop's former house seven years earlier, they had discovered "several small poppets [dolls] made of rags and hog bristles" with pins sticking out of them hidden in the building's foundation.[12] Witches were said to fashion dolls in the likeness of their victims. When a witch harmed a doll—by stabbing it with pins, typically—her human victim would supposedly also be harmed.

The court testimony of the two laborers was especially incriminating since it involved physical evidence of witchcraft. Yet, "as damning as this physical evidence of Bishop's occult activities seemed, the decisive factor in her case, as it would be in all those convicted, was spectral evidence," observes Larry Gragg.[13] A remarkably large and diverse group of people claimed to have encountered Bishop's spectral form over the years, including numerous adult neighbors and acquaintances in addition to the core band of "afflicted girls," including Ann Putnam, Mercy Lewis, and Abigail Williams. Among Bishop's adult accusers was Samuel Gray. Fourteen years earlier, Gray reported, he had awakened from a sound sleep to discover the specter of a woman hovering over his baby's cradle. Soon after, the child died. Although he was unable to identify the specter at the time, Gray testified that he was now sure it was Bishop's form he had seen by his infant's bed on that long-ago night.

After all the witnesses had finished testifying, Bishop was finally given the opportunity to defend herself before the court. (Bishop had no lawyer to argue her case for her, because witchcraft defendants were not permitted to hire legal counsel.) The jury was unconvinced by Bridget's repeated declarations of innocence. How long they deliberated has been lost to history, but Bridget was found guilty of witchcraft and sentenced to die. On the morning of June 10, the Essex County sheriff and several guards transported Bishop by cart to a desolate, rocky hill on Salem's western boundary. Bridget Bishop, who maintained her innocence to the very end, was blindfolded and, in accordance with the warrant issued for her by Chief Justice Stoughton, "hanged by the neck until . . . dead."[14] By the end of the summer, 18 other accused witches had been hanged on the same rocky hillside, earning the barren promontory the macabre nickname "Gallows Hill."

A Deadly Panic

The first trial and hanging of the Salem witchcraft crisis brought a brief lull in the frantic pace of the witch hunt. During the weeks immediately following the execution of Bridget Bishop, the number of accusations plummeted. "Perhaps the elimination of an important suspect brought a sense of relief, a generalized lowering of tension; or perhaps some participants were sobered by the high stakes of what they were about," writes John Demos.[1] At the same time, it appeared that William Phips and his Council (a governmental body responsible for advising the governor in judicial and other matters) were having some doubts regarding how the witchcraft emergency had been handled thus far. A few days after Bishop's execution, they asked more than a dozen of the colony's most respected Puritan ministers, including Cotton and Increase Mather, for their thoughts "upon the present witchcraft in Salem."[2]

THE MINISTERS WEIGH IN

On June 15, the clergymen presented Governor Phips and his Council with a long report evaluating the first full-fledged witch trial as well as the dozens of preliminary examinations held in Salem over the previous four months. Entitled "The Return [Reply] of Several Ministers Consulted," the ministers' assessment of the proceedings was strikingly ambivalent. On the one hand, the report praised the magistrates for their piety and perseverance in striving to defend the people of Massachusetts from the evil power of Satan and his earthly servants. On the other, it raised unsettling questions regarding some of the judges' actions.

After opening the report with glowing praise for "the sedulous and assiduous endeavors of our honorable rulers to detect the abominable witch-crafts which have been committed in the country," the authors of "The Return" expressed several misgivings about the conduct of the legal proceedings to date.[3] Obviously worried that the witch hunt was ensnaring too many community members "of formerly unblemished reputation"— persons such as beloved matriarch Rebecca Nurse, or wealthy merchant Philip English, for example—the ministers admonished the Court of Oyer and Terminer to use "exceeding tenderness" in prosecuting the accused.[4] Specifically, they warned against two folk tests for detecting witches that had been widely employed in the pretrial hearings: the touch and the Lord's Prayer tests. Satan could easily manipulate both tests to confuse the faithful and gain "an advantage over us," the clergymen cautioned.[5] In the first test, the defendant was commanded to touch their accuser while he or she was in the throes of a fit. Supposedly, if the specter of the defendant was causing the afflicted person's suffering, the victim's torments would stop as soon as the offending witch made physical contact with her or him. In the second test, the accused was instructed to recite the Lord's Prayer in front of the courtroom. Because witches were thought to be incapable of reciting the prayer perfectly,

Difficulties arose in the witchcraft trials because it was believed that Satan could manipulate evidence and tests. The judges were cautioned against accepting spectral testimony, a warning that they ignored.

any error made by the defendant, no matter how trivial, was considered as evidence of guilt.

Of all the ministers' reservations regarding the court's handling of the witchcraft crisis, however, the most serious was the magistrates' heavy reliance on spectral testimony. The problem with such evidence, they argued, was that Satan conceivably could take the shape of "an innocent . . . and a virtuous man" without his permission or knowledge. Consequently, they warned, judges should exercise "a very critical and exquisite caution" regarding spectral testimony lest they be misled by "things received only upon the Devil's authority."[6]

The ministers were going out on a limb by criticizing the reliability of spectral evidence. Not only had such evidence played a central role in all the pretrial examinations and in Bridget Bishop's conviction, but Lieutenant Governor Stoughton, the second-highest political authority in Massachusetts, was widely known to be a staunch believer in its usefulness. The Court of Oyer and Terminer's chief justice considered spectral evidence completely reliable because he was convinced that God would never allow Satan to assume the image of an innocent person.

Despite their willingness to raise troublesome questions regarding spectral testimony and certain folk tests, the ministers seemed to have lost their nerve entirely by the end of the report. Presumably out of fear of offending Stoughton and the other influential magistrates of the Court of Oyer and Terminer, the authors of "The Return" closed their evaluation of the Salem proceedings "with words that undermine everything so far written," observes Frances Hill.[7] Going back to the unqualified support for the judges with which they had opened their report, the clergymen concluded: "Nevertheless, we cannot but humbly recommend unto the Government the speedy and vigorous prosecution of such as have rendered themselves obnoxious, according to the direction given in the law of God, and the wholesome statues of the English nation, for the detection of witchcrafts."[8] The effect of the ministers' final statement, asserts Hill,

> was to give Stoughton and his court the ministers' seal of approval. The judges could not prosecute speedily and vigorously except by employing the methods they had already been using, including spectral evidence. Unless the ministers followed up their strictures about the need for caution and set aside their recommendations for vigor and speed, it was inevitable that juries would continue to sentence them to death. They would do so on the evidence that had damned

the accused at their examinations, that is, the afflicted girls' tortures. The *Return* would not impede the course of events but encourage it. The ministers wanted to voice their misgivings without opposing the judges. If they had been wholehearted about the unreliability of spectral evidence, they would have suggested barring the girls from the courtroom. Then the cases against most of the accused witches would have collapsed and the trials would have ceased. But the ministers chose to be swept along by a dangerous tide instead of trying to stem it. . . . None of the ministers, however great their unease, wanted to step out of line.[9]

THE TRIALS RESUME

On June 28, Chief Justice Stoughton reconvened the Court of Oyer and Terminer for its second full session—with one change in its makeup. Magistrate Nathaniel Saltonstall had resigned from the court shortly after Bridget Bishop's trial, presumably out of dissatisfaction with the central role of spectral testimony in her conviction. None of the other judges gave any indication that they shared Saltonstall's misgivings; indeed, spectral evidence would play a key role in every one of the more than two-dozen trials that the judges oversaw during the next three months.

Clearly taking to heart the ministers' recommendation that they act with speed and vigor in prosecuting the accused, the court tried five defendants between June 28 and June 30. They included Salem Village residents Sarah Good and Rebecca Nurse, and three women from neighboring communities: Topsfield residents Elizabeth Howe and Sarah Wildes, and Susannah Martin of Amesbury. All five were convicted and condemned to die on the same sort of evidence used against Bishop. This included the alleged torments of their accusers, especially Ann Putnam, Abigail Williams, Mercy Lewis, and the other "afflicted girls"; the misfortunes suffered by neighbors and acquaintances with whom they had quarreled; the presence

The witch trials proceeded swiftly during June and July 1692, with a total of six women convicted and condemned to die.

of "witch marks" on their bodies; and, last but not least, the testimony of witchcraft confessors.

Since Tituba's dramatic confession in March, several other accused persons also claimed to have signed the devil's book and attended secret witch meetings. Among these confessors were Deliverance Hobbs of Topsfield and her teenage daughter, Abigail, and John and Elizabeth Proctor's 20-year-old maidservant, Mary Warren. Warren had started out as one of the chief Salem Village accusers along with Ann Putnam and Abigail Williams. But as more and more suspected witches were hauled off to jail, she apparently had second thoughts. Blaming her own involvement in the witch hunt on temporary insanity, she declared that none of the afflicted girls' accusations ought to be taken seriously. Shortly afterward, Mary herself became the target of witchcraft accusations when several of the afflicted girls claimed that Warren's specter had attacked them. Under intense and prolonged questioning by Salem authorities, Mary confessed to witchcraft. Many historians believe that her confession was prompted by a desire to protect herself by telling her interrogators what they seemed to want to hear and agreeing to provide evidence against other witch suspects. If that was in fact Mary's intention, the ploy worked remarkably well. Warren's apparently heartfelt repentance and active participation in the prosecution of other accused witches, including her former employers, the Proctors, so ingratiated her to the magistrates that they ordered her release from prison in June 1692. Deliverance and Abigail Hobbs, Tituba, and the other witchcraft confessors were not as fortunate: They all remained in prison. Nonetheless, not a single one of the confessors was executed during the course of the Salem trials, presumably because of their usefulness in testifying against other accused witches.

"FULL OF GRIEF"

Of the five trials held at the end of June, the one that received the most attention from the Salem community was Rebecca Nurse's on June 29. The 71-year-old matriarch's arrest the previous spring had aroused angry protests from her family members and numerous friends. Forty of Rebecca's supporters had signed a petition on her behalf prepared by her husband, despite the possible risks to themselves. "We can testify that we have known [Rebecca Nurse] for many years, . . . and we never had any cause or grounds to suspect her of any such thing as she is now accused of," the petition declared.[10]

The testimony of Nurse's numerous loyal backers in Salem seems to have made an impression on the jury, because they cleared her of all charges. Yet no sooner had the verdict been announced than Nurse's accusers began to shriek and moan so loudly that the entire courtroom was thrown into an uproar. After several magistrates expressed concern regarding the well-being of the afflicted girls, Stoughton asked the jury to reconsider their finding. Specifically, the chief justice urged them to reexamine what Nurse had declared when Deliverance and Abigail Hobbs first entered the courtroom to testify against her, words that could be interpreted as implying a prior bond between herself and the two confessed witches. "What, do these persons give evidence against me now, they used to come among us," Rebecca had exclaimed.

When, at Stoughton's prompting, the jury foreman asked Nurse to clarify her statement, however, she only stared at him blankly and said nothing. Taking this as an admission of guilt, the jury reversed their verdict. What the jury failed to realize was that, nearly deaf and beside herself with anxiety, Nurse had never heard the foreman's question in the first place, as she later explained to the court in a letter. If she had heard the foreman's query, Nurse assured the magistrates, she would have answered that she had merely been expressing her surprise that her former prison cellmates were testifying against her. "Hard of hearing and full of grief," Nurse wrote to the judges, she "had not opportunity to declare what I intended."[11] Although the court was unmoved by Nurse's protestation of innocence, her family managed to convince Governor Phips to grant Rebecca a reprieve. When the afflicted girls fell into more violent fits than ever on hearing that their alleged tormenter was to escape the hangman's noose, however, Phips quickly backed down.

On July 19, Rebecca Nurse, Sarah Good, and the other three women tried during the second session of the Court of Oyer and Terminer, were hanged in the first mass execution of witches in British America. The widely publicized execution "produced a tumultuous scene," writes John Demos. A large throng, including several of the afflicted girls, gathered on Gallows Hill to watch the hangings. Among the crowd were several local ministers, including one of the witch hunt's most fanatical supporters, the Reverend Nicholas Noyes of Salem Town. Noyes's unsuccessful attempt to coax a last-minute confession from feisty Sarah Good "brought a scathing—and unforgettable—retort," Demos reports. "I am no more a witch than you are a wizard," Good shot back at the shocked minister, "and if you take away my life God will give you blood to drink."[12] According to Salem tradition, Good's gruesome prophecy was fulfilled 25 years later when Noyes suffered an internal hemorrhage and died gagging on his own blood.

THE CRISIS INTENSIFIES

Shortly after the second round of witchcraft trials resulted in convictions—and death sentences—for all five defendants, Jacob Melijn, a Dutch merchant living in Boston, wrote a letter to an acquaintance in New York, decrying the Salem proceedings. Melijn was particularly disgusted with the "the gullibility of the magistrates" in permitting "trivial circumstances to be taken as substantially true and convincing testimony against the accused."[13] The entire witchcraft crisis, Melijn was convinced, was rooted in "superstition and mistakes."[14] As the month of July proceeded, however, it appeared that few residents of Salem or neighboring communities shared Melijn's views, or if they did, they were afraid to voice them publicly.

By the time of the July 19 executions, the lull in new accusations that had followed Bridget Bishop's death was already over, and the witch panic had come back with a vengeance to Essex County. The hardest-hit community outside of Salem Village was the town of Andover. Andover's witch hunt had begun in mid-July, when resident Joseph Ballard had asked several of the afflicted girls in nearby Salem Village to visit his ill wife. Ballard suspected that his wife had been bewitched and wanted the girls to help identify her tormentors. Happy to oblige, the girls identified five Andover residents as witches. Soon after their visit, the town acquired its own group of afflicted. Between July 15 and late August, their testimony helped send 40 of their fellow townspeople—10 percent of the town's population—to jail on witchcraft charges.

On August 5, the Court of Oyer and Terminer met for its third full session in Salem. Six defendants were tried: John and Elizabeth Proctor and farmer John Willard of Salem Village; elderly George Jacobs of Salem Town; housewife Martha Carrier of Andover; and a former pastor of the Salem Village church, George Burroughs. Shortly after the July 19 executions, an imprisoned John Proctor had written a letter to five of the city's leading ministers, including Increase Mather. In the letter, Proctor begged the ministers to convince Governor Phips to replace Stoughton and the other judges on the court, contending that they were biased against him and the other suspects and had "condemned us already before our trials." He also complained that torture was being used to force confessions from some of the prisoners, including Martha Carrier's two teenage sons. The boys had confessed to witchcraft and reported seeing Proctor and several of the other defendants at a witch meeting, Proctor wrote, only after their jailers had tied them "neck and heels." His own son received the same cruel treatment when he was questioned, Proctor added: "My son William Proctor . . . because he would not confess that he was guilty . . . they tied him neck and heels till the blood gushed out of his nose, and would have kept him so 24 hours, if one more merciful than the rest had not taken pity on him and caused him to be unbound."[15]

Proctor's pleas for intervention from the clergy on behalf of himself and the approximately 100 other witch suspects being held in Essex County jails fell on deaf ears. The composition and proceedings of the Court of Oyer and Terminer remained unchanged, and on August 5, Proctor, his wife, and the four others tried that day were found guilty of witchcraft. After George Jacobs was sentenced to die on August 19, one of the chief witnesses for the prosecution, his 17-year-old granddaughter, Margaret, made a desperate, last-ditch effort to save him. Margaret had agreed to testify against her grandfather only after being accused of practicing witchcraft herself. The night before Jacobs's execution, she recanted her testimony against him, but to no avail. The only one of the six defendants in the third round of trials to escape the hangman's noose was Elizabeth Proctor, who was awarded a stay of execution because she was pregnant. (As it turned out, Elizabeth's death sentence was never carried out. In May 1693, five months after giving birth to a son, John Proctor Jr., she was released from prison.)

REVEREND GEORGE BURROUGHS

The executions of August 19 attracted the largest and most distinguished audience of any of the hangings on Gallows Hill to date, with five Massachusetts ministers in attendance, including Cotton Mather. The intense interest in the August 19 executions centered on the Reverend George Burroughs, the only clergyman ever to be charged in the Salem crisis and the alleged ringleader of all the Massachusetts witches.

The son of a well-to-do Puritan merchant, Burroughs graduated from Harvard in 1670. After serving as a frontier pastor in Maine for 10 years, he accepted an offer to lead the Salem Village church in 1680. But his tenure at Salem was cut short by a bitter financial squabble with some of his parishioners, particularly members of the Putnam family, and in 1683, he returned to Maine. In April 1692, Ann Putnam, who had undoubtedly heard about Burroughs from her older relatives, accused the Maine pastor of being the head of the witch cult that was supposedly threatening eastern Massachusetts. After several of the other afflicted girls joined Putnam in accusing Burroughs of practicing malevolent magic, including bewitching his first two wives to death, Salem authorities traveled to Maine to arrest the 39-year-old minister and father of five. At his August 5 trial, eight confessing witches accused Burroughs of acting as the high priest at their clandestine meetings. Other witnesses, acquaintances of Burroughs in Maine, claimed to

George Burroughs was the only clergyman ever to be charged in the witchcraft trials. Convicted as ringleader of all the Massachusetts witches, Burroughs was executed on August 19, 1692.

have observed the minister performing feats of superhuman strength such as lifting a heavy barrel of molasses with only two fingers. Throughout the trial, Burroughs repeatedly and passionately protested his innocence, even going so far as to submit a written statement to the jury arguing "that there neither are, nor ever were witches," according to a later account of the proceedings by Cotton Mather.[16]

Burroughs continued to insist on his innocence to the last. His evident sincerity and courageous dignity made a deep impression on many in the large throng that gathered on Gallows Hill to witness his hanging on August 19. As he was about to be executed, Burroughs "made a speech . . . with such solemn and serious expressions as were to the admiration of all

COTTON MATHER

Cotton Mather was born on February 12, 1663, in Boston. His father, Increase Mather, was one of Massachusetts's best-known and beloved clergymen, and his maternal grandfather, John Cotton, who immigrated to Boston from England in 1633, was the leading Puritan preacher of New England's founding generation. A brilliant child, by the time he turned 12, Mather had been admitted to Harvard College. He earned his bachelor's degree at age 15, receiving his master's 3 years later. After being ordained as a clergyman in 1685, Mather joined his father as co-minister of New England's largest congregation, the Second Church of Boston. One year later, he married Abigail Phillips, and in August 1687, the couple's first child, a daughter, was born. The infant's death four months later was to be the first in a long series of personal tragedies suffered by Mather. By the time he died in 1728 at age 65, Mather had outlived two wives and 13 of the 15 children he fathered by them.

Over the centuries since his death, Cotton Mather's association with the notorious Salem witchcraft trials has tended to overshadow his many scholarly and scientific achievements. One of colonial America's most prolific writers, Mather published nearly 450 pam-

present," wrote Boston merchant Robert Calef in his highly critical account of the Salem trials published in 1700, *More Wonders
of the Invisible World.* "His prayer," reported Calef, "was so well
worded, and uttered with such . . . fervency of spirit as was very
affecting and drew tears from many, so that it seemed to some
that the spectators would hinder the execution." At that crucial
moment, Cotton Mather, who harbored no doubts whatsoever
regarding Burroughs's guilt, spoke out, reminding the restless

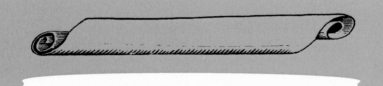

phlets and books during his lifetime on a wide range of subjects
including theology, history, science, and music. Mather has also
been lauded as the father of American medicine for his central role
in promoting smallpox inoculation. One of the most dreaded diseases of the colonial era, smallpox typically killed one in five of its victims. Nonetheless, when Mather, who had read about the successful
use of smallpox inoculations in Turkey, spearheaded a campaign
to inoculate Bostonians with fluid from smallpox blisters during an
outbreak in 1721, his fellow townspeople turned on him with a vengeance. Convinced that the inoculations would only spread the dis-
ease further, one panicky Bostonian even hurled a homemade bomb
through the window of Mather's house. But Mather persisted with
his inoculations, and when the results of his bold experiment were
in, the death rate among inoculated Bostonians was found to be
significantly lower than among those who had contracted smallpox
naturally. Mather's successful experiment helped gain widespread
acceptance for smallpox inoculation in the American colonies and
Europe and paved the way for the development of a safer smallpox
vaccine in the late 1700s.

crowd that the wily prince of darkness, Satan, "had often been transformed into an angel of light."[17] Mather's words swayed the onlookers enough so that the executions were able to continue. Immediately after the hangings, Burroughs's corpse and those of the four others who died with him were thrown into a common grave, which had been so hastily dug that the minister's chin and one of his hands were left uncovered, according to Calef. Historian John Demos observed that, "Even in death, a witch deserved the utmost ignominy [disgrace]."[18]

Growing Doubts

The August 19 executions marked a turning point in the Salem witchcraft crisis. The crowd's sympathetic response to Reverend Burroughs's final words provided the first indication of significant doubt among the general public regarding the guilt of at least some of the convicted. As the summer of 1692 drew to a close, however, it was evident that the judges of the Court of Oyer and Terminer did not share those doubts. The next round of witchcraft trials in September 1692 would result in the largest number of convictions—and executions— thus far.

THE SEPTEMBER TRIALS

Over a period of 12 days in September, the Court of Oyer and Terminer tried 13 women and 2 men for witchcraft. By September 17, when the fourth series of trials ended, all 15 had been convicted and condemned to hang. They were: Martha Corey and Abigail Hobbs of Salem Village; Ann Pudeator and Alice Parker of Salem Town; Mary Easty of Topsfield; Dorcas Hoar of Beverly; Mary Bradbury of Salisbury; Margaret Scott of Rowley; Wilmott Redd of Marblehead; and Mary Parker, Abigail Faulkner, Mary Lacy, Ann Foster, Rebecca Eames, and Samuel Wardwell of Andover.

Ultimately, 7 of the 15 sentenced to die for the crime of witchcraft in September would escape execution. Abigail Faulkner was granted a reprieve because she was pregnant. Mary Bradbury, the elderly wife of one of Salisbury's leading citizens, magistrate Thomas Bradbury, escaped from prison, probably by bribing her jailer. (There were other escapees as well, including Philip and Mary English and another prominent Massachusetts resident, John Alden of Boston. A well-off merchant and sea captain, Alden was the son of Pilgrim settlers John and Priscilla Mullins Alden, whose romance aboard the *Mayflower* was immortalized by the nineteenth-century poet Henry Wadsworth Longfellow in *The Courtship of Miles Standish.*) Dorcas Hoar, Mary Lacy, Abigail Hobbs, Ann Foster, and Rebecca Eames—all confessed witches—received stays of execution, presumably so they could continue to testify in court against other defendants.

A sixth confessor tried in September, Samuel Wardwell, a carpenter and farmer from Andover, was not so fortunate. In a lengthy and detailed confession made during his preliminary examination on September 1, Wardwell claimed to have signed the devil's book and tormented his chief accuser, 16-year-old Martha Sprague of Andover, in exchange for a more comfortable life. Additionally, he accused two suspects from Reading, Massachusetts—Mary Taylor and Jane Lilly—of being witches. During his trial, Wardwell had an abrupt change of heart, however. He recanted his entire confession, admitting that he had "belyed himselfe" (perjured himself) and "he knew he should dye [die] for it: whether he owned it or no."[1]

Wardwell's case is notable not only because he recanted his confession but also for what it reveals about the financial and emotional consequences of the Salem crisis for many of the accused witches' families. The situation of the Wardwell family was particularly desperate because Samuel's wife, Sarah, was also thrown in jail on charges of witchcraft in early September, leaving the couple's five youngest children on their own. A petition filed by the selectman of Andover that month regarding the Wardwell children provides a sad reminder of the heavy toll that long imprisonments could exact from a suspect's dependents:

> Samuel Wardwell and his wife of Andover were lately appre-hended and committed to prison for witchcraft, and have left several small children who are incapable of providing for themselves and are now in a suffering condition. We have thought it necessary and convenient that they should be disposed of in some families whether there may be due care taken of them. We therefore humbly pray your honors to inform us what is our duty in this case.[2]

NINE MORE EXECUTIONS

Wardwell and the seven other convicted witches whose death sentences had not been commuted were scheduled to hang on September 22. Three days before their appointed execu-tion day, a ninth accused witch, Martha Corey's 72-year-old husband, Giles, was executed in a particularly shocking and grisly way for refusing to enter a plea of innocent or guilty before the bar. Corey, who was known for his quick temper and pigheadedness, insisted that it was pointless for him to stand trial. Although he had never practiced witchcraft, the court was certain to convict him anyway, he declared. After all, Corey pointed out, not a single person tried by the Court of Oyer and Terminer since its creation three months earlier had been found innocent. Determined to make Corey cooperate,

The Salem Witch Trials Memorial stands next to the Old Burying Point Cemetary in Salem, Massachusetts.

the court ordered that he be tortured using an ancient English procedure called *peine forte et dure* (strong and hard punishment). Corey was forced to lie flat on the ground while "great weights"—probably heavy rocks—were piled on his chest.[3] Corey was warned that weight would continue to be added until he either agreed to enter a plea or died. The elderly farmer stubbornly endured hours of this savage treatment before finally succumbing. According to Salem tradition, Corey's only words throughout the ordeal were "more weight."[4]

"Since pressing to death had never been practiced before in New England," contends Frances Hill, Corey's gruesome death "had an extremely unsettling effect on the populace."[5] According to contemporary accounts, so, too, did the hangings of Ann Pudeator, Mary Easty, Margaret Scott, Wilmott Redd, Samuel Wardwell, Mary Parker, Alice Parker, and Martha Corey on September 22. During the solemn final prayers and farewells of the condemned, "tears [flowed] from the eyes of almost all present," wrote Robert Calef. One of the few completely unsympathetic onlookers on September 22 was the Reverend Nicholas Noyes of Salem. Immediately after the executions, Noyes contemptuously declared: "What a sad thing it is to see eight firebrands of hell hanging there!"[6] The minister's scornful attitude toward the deceased "may have had the contrary effect to what he intended, stirring opposition to the hangings," rather than support, suggests Hill. "The crowd may have been no more restive than at George Burroughs's execution," she

THE PETITION OF MARY EASTY

At the time that she was sentenced to death for witchcraft in September 1692, Mary Easty was 58 years old. Married to a farmer from Topsfield, a small community just north of Salem Village, she was the mother of seven. Like her sisters Rebecca Nurse, who was hanged in July, and Sarah Cloyce, who had been imprisoned on charges of witchcraft since March but had yet to stand trial, Easty was a regular churchgoer and respected member of her community.

On the eve of her execution on September 22, Easty wrote an eloquent petition to Governor Phips and the judges of the Court of Oyer and Terminer in support of the estimated 155 witchcraft suspects, including her sister Sarah, then languishing in jail. Although careful to avoid criticizing the motives or piety of the judges, Easty pled with the magistrates to reconsider whether their apparently

(continues)

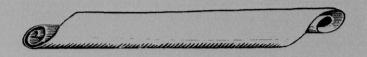

(continued)

unwavering faith in the integrity of the afflicted girls and the confessing witches was justified:

> I petition to your Honors not for my own life, for I know I must die, and the appointed time is set; but . . . if it be possible, that no more innocent blood be shed, which undoubtedly cannot be avoided in the way and course you go in. I question too, not but your Honors do to the utmost of your powers in the discovery and detecting of witchcraft and witches, and would not be guilty of innocent blood for the world; but by my own innocency, I know you are in the wrong way. The Lord in his infinite mercy direct you in this great work, that innocent blood be not shed; I would humbly beg of your Honors would be pleased to examine some of those confessing witches, I being confident several of them have belied themselves and others, as will appear, if not in this world, . . .in the world to come, whither I am going; and I question not, but your selves will see an alteration in these things. They say, myself and others have made a league with the Devil, we cannot confess. I know and the Lord knows (as will shortly appear) they belie me, and so I question not but they do others; the Lord alone, who is the searcher of all hearts, as I shall answer at the Tribunal Seat, that I know not the least thing of witchcraft, therefore I cannot, I durst not belie my own soul. I beg your Honors not to deny this my humble petition, from a poor, dying, and innocent person, and I question not but the Lord will give a blessing to your endeavors.*

---

* Quoted in Larry Dale Gragg, *The Salem Witchcraft Crisis*. New York: Praeger, 1992,pp. 165--166.

writes, "but there was perhaps a sense, by the time the eight were 'hanging there,' that it had at last had its fill."[7]

GROWING CRITICISM OF THE TRIALS

While many ordinary citizens were becoming uneasy with the court's handling of the increasingly deadly witchcraft crisis during the late summer of 1692, the trials were also beginning to attract some prominent critics. Among these were the Boston merchant and scientist Thomas Brattle and two leading Boston ministers, Samuel Willard and Increase Mather.

Sometime during the early autumn of 1692, Willard composed and distributed a manuscript on the witchcraft panic entitled "Some Miscellany Observations on Our Present Debates Respecting Witchcrafts: A Dialogue Between 'S' And 'B.'" In it, Willard blasted the court's reliance on spectral evidence and the testimony of confessors like Tituba or Abigail Hobbs in convicting defendants. If the confessors were indeed witches, as they claimed to be, it would be the height of naïveté for the magistrates to place any trust in their testimony, Willard pointed out. Since by signing Satan's book, they had "given themselves up to the Devil, the father of lies," Willard insisted, no credence "should be given to the testimony of such against the lives of others."[8]

In early October, Increase Mather, the most esteemed and influential clergyman in Massachusetts, launched his own attack on the court's use of spectral evidence. Mather had expressed doubts regarding such evidence in the *Return of Several Ministers* more than three months earlier, following the first execution of the witchcraft crisis. Since then, however, he, along with the vast majority of his clerical colleagues in New England, had remained quiet regarding the Salem proceedings. On October 3, Mather finally broke his silence in a sermon preached before a gathering of Puritan ministers in Cambridge, Massachusetts. In his address, which was soon published under the title *Cases of Conscience Concerning Evil Spirits Personating*

Increase Mather, Massachusetts's most prominent clergyman, believed that spectral evidence should be given no credence in the witch trials. His published address stating his opinion regarding the unreliability of such evidence was so influential that clergy and other leaders began to turn against the witch trials.

Men, Mather argued that the evidence in witchcraft cases "ought to be as clear as in any other crimes of a capital nature." Yet, he contended, the spectral testimony that had helped convict most of the condemned in the Salem trials was far from clear-cut. Like Willard, Mather believed Satan could almost certainly appear in the shape of an innocent man or woman to serve his own evil ends. Moreover, because only the afflicted person could see his or her spectral attackers, spectral testimony was virtually impossible to verify, Mather asserted. "It were better that ten suspected witches should escape, than that one innocent person should be condemned," he concluded dramatically, adding, "I had rather judge a witch to be an honest woman, than judge an honest woman as a witch."[9]

COTTON MATHER WEIGHS IN

Fourteen prominent Massachusetts clergymen, including Samuel Willard, formally endorsed Increase Mather's condemnation of spectral evidence by signing the preface to the *Cases of Conscience*. Notably missing from the list was Increase's son, Cotton Mather. Shortly after *Cases of Conscience* appeared in print, Cotton Mather published a work of his own on the witchcraft trials, a book that stood in stark contrast to his father's tract. Entitled *The Wonders of the Invisible World*, Mather's analysis of the trials strongly defended the actions of the Court of Oyer and Terminer.

Mather had begun researching *The Wonders of the Invisible World*, which featured accounts of five of the trials, including those of Bridget Bishop and George Burroughs, in September. Given the enormity of Satan's threat to the godly people of New England, he insisted in his book that the extraordinary number of witchcraft convictions and executions in Salem during the summer of 1692 were completely justified. Although *The Wonders of the Invisible World* was publicly endorsed by Lieutenant Governor Stoughton, in defending the Salem proceedings, observes John Demos, Mather "was swimming against a steadily rising tide." In common with Cotton's father, most New England ministers—and many governmental leaders as well—had come to the conclusion that the proceedings needed to be thoroughly reexamined before any more defendants were brought to court. "The momentum for prosecution did not collapse all at once," writes Demos, but by the time Mather's book was published in October, the Salem trials had become so controversial that even Governor Phips had turned against them.[10]

Phips had just returned to Boston from a six-week-long visit to the war-torn Maine frontier when Increase and Cotton Mather's very different takes on the witchcraft trials went to press. The governor was presented with both works, but he clearly found the older Mather's critique of the trials considerably more persuasive than the younger one's defense of them. Most historians agree it was Increase's carefully reasoned criticism of the proceedings, together with an alarming increase in the number of prominent persons being named as witches, which convinced Phips to suspend the Court of Oyer and Terminer on October 12, and finally dissolve the tribunal altogether on October 29. (According to some accounts, by the time that Phips returned to Boston from Maine in late September, the growing ranks of prominent citizens accused of witchcraft had even come to include the governor's own wife, Lady Mary Spencer Phips, although she was never arrested.)

THE END OF THE SALEM WITCHCRAFT TRIALS

After a two-month hiatus, the witchcraft trials reconvened in Salem in early 1693. But this time the atmosphere surrounding the trials, which were to be conducted by the recently established Superior Court of Judicature, was quite different than during the previous June, when the Court of Oyer and Terminer had first convened in Salem. "Within just a few short weeks in October 1692 a considerable share of the once-significant support for the trials seems to have evaporated," writes Mary Beth Norton.[11] Relatives and friends of many of the approximately 150 people still imprisoned wrote petitions urging that their loved ones be released at once; a steadily growing number of witch confessors recanted their earlier testimony; and one of the alleged witchcraft victims, 17-year-old Mary Herrick of Wenham, admitted that her afflictions had likely been nothing more than "a delusion of the Devil."[12] Herrick also informed her pastor, the Reverend Joseph Gerrish, and the Reverend John Hale of Beverly that Mary Easty's ghost had appeared to her and declared that she was innocent of witchcraft and had been wrongly executed.

The five judges appointed by Governor Phips to sit on the Superior Court of Judicature began hearing witchcraft cases on January 3, 1693. The court consisted of Chief Justice Stoughton and four associate justices: Samuel Sewall, John Richards, Waitsill Winthrop, and Thomas Danforth, the former deputy governor of Massachusetts. Even though Stoughton was still in charge of the witchcraft proceedings and all but one of his fellow magistrates (Danforth) were holdovers from the Court of Oyer and Terminer, the judges were to be guided by new rules of evidence authorized by Governor Phips. Most significantly, spectral evidence was now impermissible.

As a direct result of the new policy regarding spectral evidence, charges were dismissed against approximately two-dozen defendants being held in Salem and Boston prisons, before their cases even went to trial. Among this group was Sarah Cloyce, the sister of Mary Easty and Rebecca Nurse. Another 21 defendants were indicted by a grand jury and tried by the Superior Court in early January, but just three were found guilty: Mary Post of Rowley and Andover residents Elizabeth Johnson Jr. and Sarah Wardwell. Chief Justice Stoughton issued death warrants for the trio and for five other defendants who had been found guilty during the summer by the Court of Oyer and Terminer, but whose executions had been delayed. This latter group included Elizabeth Proctor and Abigail Faulkner, both of whom had recently given birth, and several confessors. But to Stoughton's dismay, Phips reprieved all of the condemned until the king's attorney for Massachusetts could review their

The Rebecca Nurse Homestead in Danvers, Massachusetts.

cases. On his advice, Phips decided to revoke the Chief Justice's execution orders just one day before the hangings were to take place. According to Phips, Stoughton was so "enraged and filled with passionate anger" by the governor's interference, that he initially refused to participate in the second round of witchcraft trials held by the Superior Court in Charlestown, Massachusetts, in February 1693.[13]

At the February session, and at two more sessions of the court held in Boston and Ipswich, respectively, in late April and mid-May 1693, a total of 10 witchcraft defendants were tried and found innocent. The May session of the Superior Court signaled the end of the witchcraft trials when grand juries dismissed charges against all the remaining suspects. At Phips's order, all accused witches still in jail were discharged, pending payment of prison fees. Among this group was Samuel Parris's slave, Tituba. Tituba, who recanted her dramatic confession of March 1692 before her release, remained in prison for nearly 14 months, longer than any other defendant in the witchcraft crisis. On her release, Parris promptly sold Tituba to a new, out-of-town owner, and the woman who had played such a vital role in the development of the Salem witchcraft panic disappeared forever from the written record.

Aftermath and Legacy

The people of Massachusetts struggled for years to put the deadliest witch hunt in American history behind them. Not until 1711 would the Massachusetts government admit its responsibility for the lethal trials and make financial restitution to the victims' families. By then, as public opinion turned ever more strongly against the trials, several of the jurors, ministers, and others whose words and deeds had helped bring about the imprisonment of some 155 suspects and the deaths of at least 25 persons had publicly apologized for their roles in the crisis. Nearly two decades after the trials ended, the healing process could finally begin in earnest. (Regarding the final death toll of 25: In addition to the 20 who were executed in Salem, at least 5 others, including Sarah Good's infant child, died in prison.)

REVEREND PARRIS TRIES TO MAKE AMENDS

The first major figure in the Salem witch crisis to express regret for his part in the deadly episode was Samuel Parris, one of the primary instigators of the witch hunt. Reverend Parris made his public apology in late 1694, a year and a half after Governor Phips ordered the release of all witchcraft suspects still in prison. Most historians agree that Parris's willingness to admit that he may have been mistaken—or at least, overly zealous—in the witch persecutions was motivated above all by a desire to hold onto his Salem Village pulpit.

Parris had been fighting to keep his job for nearly two years before the witchcraft frenzy erupted in his household in the early winter of 1692. A group of disgruntled parishioners led by the Porter family had been trying to oust Parris ever since he was granted full ownership of the parsonage in 1690 over their objections. What made Parris's victory in the parsonage controversy particularly irksome to the Porter faction was that it was only made possible by the support of their longtime enemies, the Putnams. For years, the Porters, backed by other commercially oriented villagers, had been locked in a bitter struggle with the Putnams and other traditional, small-scale farmers regarding whether the village should stay under the administration of Salem Town. The Porter faction wanted the village to remain under the bustling seaport's political control, while the Putnam-led faction, convinced that town officials had little regard for their more traditional economic and social values, wanted the village to become self-governing.

Since many members of the Porter faction were linked by bonds of blood or friendship to the beloved village matriarch, Rebecca Nurse, Parris's prominent role in the village witch hunt only deepened their opposition to him, while also attracting a number of new parishioners to their cause. Even before the trials ended in May 1693, some villagers with close ties to Nurse had begun refusing to attend weekly services. "In their view,

On January 14, 1697, Judge Samuel Sewall issued a public apology for his part in the witch trials. His minister read the statement, in which Sewall asked for forgiveness for his role in sending innocent people to their deaths.

several of Reverend Parris's sermons, during the crucial spring-time weeks in 1692, had expounded 'principles and practices' that greatly accelerated the rush to prosecution," writes John Demos.[1] By late November 1694, the campaign to oust Parris had gained so many supporters that the clergyman feared his days at the Salem Village church were numbered. "With his back to the wall, Parris read out in the meetinghouse a statement called 'mediations for peace,' which . . . said he may have spoken 'unadvisedly,' during the course of the witch-hunt," writes Frances Hill. "The tone was highly emotional though the admissions were minimal," she contends.[2] Parris's apology, heavily qualified though it was, seems to have placated some of his opponents. But in the end, his most persistent critics—the Porter family and several close relatives of Rebecca Nurse, including her son, Samuel—prevailed. In September 1697, Parris finally gave up his long and bitter fight to keep his pulpit and resigned.

A DOZEN JURORS AND ONE JUDGE APOLOGIZE

A little more than 2 years after Parris's public apology, 12 former jurors and 1 judge, Samuel Sewall, issued their own apologies for the trials. All 13 made public expressions of regret on January 14, 1697, a designated day of fasting and repentance in Massachusetts. The General Court had ordered the colony-wide day of prayer and penitence in response to several recent calamities, including growing casualties in the war against the French and their Indian allies and the sinking of several Massachusetts trading vessels. Traditionally, the Puritans interpreted such afflictions as punishments from God for their unrepented sins. On January 14, the General Court admonished the people of Massachusetts to particularly seek God's pardon for any miscarriages of justice that may have occurred during "the late [recent] tragedy raised among us by Satan and his instruments"—in other words, the Salem witchcraft trials.[4]

At the public fast day services held in Salem Town, a formal apology signed by 12 local men who had served as jurors during the trials was read aloud. Among the signers was jury foreman Thomas Fisk, who had played a central role in changing the jury's verdict from "innocent" to "guilty" at Rebecca Nurse's trial in July 1692. The jurors' statement asked for forgiveness from the Almighty, "the living sufferers," and all persons "whom we have justly offended, and do declare according to our present minds, we would none of us do such things again on such grounds for the whole world."[4] In retrospect, the jurors declared, they now realized that they had been "sadly deluded and mistaken" in many of their actions during the deadly summer of 1692.[5]

During fast day services at his church in Boston, former witchcraft judge Samuel Sewall also asked his minister to read

SAMUEL SEWALL

Born in Bishopstoke, England, on March 28, 1652, Samuel Sewall immigrated to Massachusetts with his family when he was still a young child. After earning his bachelor's degree from Harvard, Sewall married Hannah Hull, a member of one of Massachusetts's wealthiest families, in 1676. He quickly built a successful career as a merchant in Boston and also managed the colony's printing press for several years. Sewall launched his political career in 1683, when he became a member of the General Court. From 1691 to 1725, he served on the Governor's Council, advising Massachusetts's chief executive in judicial and other matters. Shortly after the Court of Oyer and Terminer was dissolved in late 1692, Sewall began a long tenure as a judge of the Superior Court of Judicature. Sewall served as chief justice of the court from 1718 until 1728, when he finally retired at age 75, two years before his death.

Today Samuel Sewall is most often remembered for his part in the notorious Salem witchcraft trials. Yet, as Eve LaPlante empha-sizes in her recent biography of Sewall, he also deserves to be aloud a letter of apology. In his statement, Sewall pled for forgiveness for his past sins, especially "the guilt contracted" from his role in the "Commission of Oyer and Terminer," for whose errors he desired "to take the blame and the shame."[7] There is every reason to believe that Sewall was genuinely repentant for his part in the witchcraft trials. For the remainder of his life, which would last for another three decades, the judge observed a private day of fasting and prayer on the anniversary of his dramatic public apology.

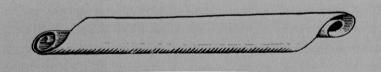

remembered as an outspoken advocate of several progressive social causes during the early eighteenth century. In 1700, Sewall authored the first antislavery tract ever published in America, "The Selling of Joseph." In direct opposition to popular social attitudes, Sewall argued in the pamphlet that slavery was immoral because God created all men equal. In keeping with his belief in the equality of all persons, regardless of race, Sewall also supported giving Native Americans more rights and educational opportunities, and he personally paid for several young Indian students to attend Harvard College. Finally, toward the end of his life, Sewall wrote a groundbreaking essay arguing for the fundamental equality of the sexes entitled "Talitha Cumi," or "Damsel, Arise."

A century and a half after his death in 1730, Sewall's diary was published in three volumes by the Massachusetts Historical Society. The judge's private journal has proven an important and fascinating source for historians of colonial America, even though Sewall said surprisingly little in his diary about the witchcraft trials.

"WE WALKED IN THE CLOUDS"

Samuel Sewall was the only Salem witchcraft judge to acknowledge that he may have made mistakes during the proceedings. Most notably, neither Chief Justice Stoughton nor John Hathorne, the most zealous of the witchcraft judges after Stoughton and an exceptionally harsh interrogator during the pretrial hearings, ever expressed the slightest remorse. "On the contrary, they stood by their actions," contends Frances Hill. "This did them no harm in their future careers. They continued as successful merchants and politicians," she observes. Hill points out that John Hathorne did eventually get his "comeuppance," when his descendant, the celebrated nineteenth-century writer Nathaniel Hawthorne, made him the model for the tyrannical witchcraft judge, Judge Pyncheon, in his novel about seventeenth-century Salem, *The House of the Seven Gables.*[7]

Most of the trials' staunchest clerical supporters also failed to apologize for their part in the witchcraft panic, with the exception of Parris and John Hale of Beverly. Hale had been an enthusiastic backer of the witch hunt until the autumn of 1692, when his wife was named as a witch. In 1697, he wrote a critical account of the trials entitled *A Modest Enquiry into the Nature of Witchcraft*. In the book, which was published in 1702, several years after his death, Hale expressed regret for his once unquestioning support of the prosecutions. Nonetheless, he also contended that he, in common with all the magistrates and others involved in the proceedings, had been motivated solely by a desire to do right. "Such was the darkness of that day, the tortures and lamentations of the afflicted, and the power of former precedents, that we walked in the clouds, and could not see our way," he wrote.[8]

Four years after the publication of Hale's book, Ann Putnam became the only one among the core group of afflicted girls to publicly apologize for her role in the witchcraft crisis. Although she was just 12 years old in 1692, Ann had been

Centuries after the witchcraft trials, this chapter in U.S. history continues to fascinate us. The Salem Witch Museum (*above*) is one of New England's most popular tourist destinations.

extremely active during the hearings and trials, naming more than 50 people in Salem Village and nearby communities as witches. In 1706, Ann, now 26 years old, asked Reverend Joseph Green of the Salem Village church to read a written statement to the congregation asking their forgiveness for her part in the witchcraft craze. Putnam, who had taken charge of her nine younger siblings after their parents' deaths seven years earlier, had recently applied for full membership in the church. "I desire to be humbled before God," Ann declared in her statement, "for the accusing of several persons of a grievous crime, whereby their lives were taken away from them, whom now I have just grounds and good reason to believe they were innocent." She had not made the accusations "out of any anger, malice, or ill-will to any person," she insisted. Rather, she had been "deceived" by a "great delusion of Satan ... whereby I justly fear I have been instrumental, with others though ignorantly and unwittingly, to bring upon myself and this land the guilt of innocent blood."[9] Despite Ann's unwillingness to accept full responsibility for her actions in 1692 by blaming them on a "delusion of Satan," the congregation clearly believed that her profession of regret was sincere, since they voted unanimously to grant Putnam membership in the church.

THE GOVERNMENT TAKES ACTION

By the early 1700s, the public apologies, along with the publication of several critical accounts of the trials, including Hale's *Modest Inquiry* and Robert Calef's *More Wonders of the Invisible World*, had emboldened many of the victims or their relations to seek justice from the government. During the first several years of the eighteenth century, the General Court received a flood of petitions on behalf of the condemned, demanding that their convictions be overturned. The names listed on the appeals included not only most of those executed on Gallows Hill but also many of the 11 convicted witches who escaped the hangman's noose, including Elizabeth Proctor and Abigail Faulkner. In her petition, Faulkner complained that, while Phips's pardon had saved her life, it had done nothing to salvage her ruined reputation or legal standing. In 1703, the General Court finally responded to the petitions by permanently outlawing the use of spectral testimony and proclaiming that "the infamy and reproach cast on the names and posterity [offspring]" of those defendants convicted because of such evidence should "in some measure be rolled away."[10] The petitioners were dismayed by the court's vaguely worded resolution. Nonetheless, they were not about to give up on their fight to restore the good names of the convicted.

Six years and numerous petitions later, a group of 22 convicted witches and relatives of the executed submitted an appeal to the General Court with a bold new demand. This time around, the petitioners asked for financial compensation from the government as well as a formal reversal of the witchcraft convictions of 1692–1993. According to Massachusetts law, prisoners had to pay for their room and board during their incarcerations. Witch suspects were also responsible for all of their court costs, including a fee for every legal document that was drawn up in relation to their prosecution. In a number of cases, local authorities confiscated household or other property from the executed or imprisoned to pay off their substantial debts to the jail keeper and court. In late 1609, several months after they submitted their appeal, the 22 petitioners gained an unexpected and highly influential ally, Cotton Mather, when the Boston minister publicly urged the General Court to meet all their financial demands.

Mather's support for the petitioners was surprising because he had never publicly apologized for his own role in the witchcraft crisis. Mather's private diary, however, reveals that by 1698, the author of the *Wonders of the Invisible World* had developed second thoughts regarding the fundamental justice of the trials. In a diary entry from January of that year, Mather fretted that the ill health several of his family members had recently suffered might be a sign of "Divine displeasure" with his actions during the Salem trials. What particularly worried him, Mather confided in his journal, was "my not appearing with vigor enough to stop the proceedings of the judges," even though he shared some of the same concerns regarding spectral evidence that his father, Increase, had expressed in October 1692 in his *Cases of Conscience.*[11]

Finally, in October 1711, the General Court approved a bill reversing the sentences of those convicted witches named in the 1709 petition. That same month, Massachusetts governor Joseph Dudley also approved financial compensation to the claimants in the amount of £578 (British pounds). On October 31, 2001, following a determined campaign on their behalf by Salem schoolteacher Paula Keene, then-governor, Jane Swift, reversed the sentences of five executed witches whose names had not been included in the 1709 petition. Among the exonerated defendants was the very first person to be hanged in the Salem panic, Bridget Bishop.

THE LEGACY OF THE SALEM WITCHCRAFT CRISIS

The most immediate consequence of the controversial Salem prosecutions was their extremely negative effect on popular attitudes toward witchcraft trials. Occasional accusations of witchcraft continued to be made in New England during the first half of the eighteenth century, but they received no backing from government authorities, the clergy, or the general populace. Many ordinary New Englanders continued to cling to traditional beliefs regarding witchcraft for decades following the trials, but no one was ever again executed as a witch in Massachusetts or anywhere in the British colonies after 1692. By the start of the Revolutionary War in 1775, the idea of diabolical witchcraft had been largely discredited throughout North America by a new, "enlightened" spirit of skepticism and faith in empirical reasoning imported from western Europe.

Few other events in the history of the United States have so captivated Americans as the Salem witchcraft trials. "The subject of scholarly tomes, films, television shows, folklore, and newspaper cartoons, and the vehicle for countless metaphors of oppression and persecution, Salem has had a powerful hold on the American imagination," observes historian Bernard Rosenthal.[12] Scholarly interest in the Salem witchcraft crisis has been particularly intense since the late twentieth century as historians, sociologists, anthropologists, and psychologists have examined the dramatic events of 1692–1693 from a variety of different perspectives. One of the most influential interpretations of the origin and course of the witch frenzy in Salem Village, home to a majority of the afflicted as well as many of the suspects, appears in Stephen Nissenbaum and Paul Boyer's *Salem Possessed*, first published in 1974. The authors' groundbreaking demographic research revealed that most of the accusers came from more traditional farming families on the western side of the village, while most of the accused villagers came from its more commercially oriented eastern side. Based on these findings, Nissenbaum and Boyer contend that the witch hunt arose out of "the resistance of back-country farmers to the pressures of commercial capitalism and the social style that accompanied it."[13] Yet, while their "argument brilliantly reveals much of the tension and underlying agendas in Salem Village," Nissenbaum and Boyer fail to explain why the witch panic spread to other Essex County communities "and caught in its net people having nothing to do with the quarrels of that particular village," points out Rosenthal.[14]

Today, most leading scholars of the trials agree that the Salem witchcraft crisis developed as a result of many different factors—external as well as internal. Among these were deep-seated popular anxieties regarding Massachusetts's uncertain political future, the increasingly violent war with the French and their Indian allies on the colony's northern frontiers, and rapid social and economic change in newly commercializing areas such as Salem Village. What is evident, however, is that not all the factors that fueled the witchcraft frenzy were unique to late seventeenth-century eastern Massachusetts. The malignant fear and intolerance that resulted in the imprisonment of more than 150 persons and the executions of 20 women and men in 1692 have resurfaced repeatedly in America and elsewhere around the globe over the past 300 years. One of the most frequently cited examples of a modern-day witch hunt is the hunt for secret Communists in the United States spearheaded by Senator Joseph McCarthy and the House Un-American

Activities Committee (HUAC) during the 1950s, when Cold War tensions were running particularly high. Arthur Miller's award-winning play of 1953 about the Salem witch panic, *The Crucible*, made a convincing parallel between the witch trials and the sensationalist hearings of HUAC, in which government officials, directors, actors, and writers reputed to hold left-wing beliefs were subpoenaed to testify before Congress. As Miller's famous play reminds us, even three centuries after they ended, the Salem witchcraft trials still teach valuable lessons about the devastating toll that malicious bigotry and exaggerated fears of hidden enemies can take on the lives and freedoms of innocent men and women.

CHRONOLOGY

1689   Samuel Parris is ordained as minister of the Salem Village church.

1692   **January** Reverend Parris's young daughter and niece start acting strangely.

February Three women, including a slave, Tituba, are accused of bewitching Parris's daughter and niece and two other village girls.

March Local magistrates question the three women, and Tituba confesses. More villagers, most of them adolescent girls, start acting bewitched. "Respectable" villagers are accused of witchcraft for the first time.

May Governor William Phips creates a Court of Oyer and Terminer to hear the growing number of witchcraft cases.

June 10 Bridget Bishop, the first to be tried by the new court, is hanged.

July 19 Five more convicted female witches are hanged in Salem.

August 19 Four men and one woman are hanged as witches.

September 19 Accused witch Giles Corey is pressed to death.

September 22 Six women and two men are hanged as witches in Salem.

October 3 Reverend Increase Mather publicly criticizes the court's use of spectral evidence in convicting accused witches.

1692   **October 29** Governor Phips dissolves the Court of Oyer and Terminer.

1693   **January–May** The Massachusetts Superior Court, after disallowing spectral evidence, tries 31 accused witches but convicts just 3 of them.

May The witchcraft trials end when Phips orders the release of all accused witches from prison.

1697   Former Salem witchcraft judge Samuel Sewall and 12 jurors publicly apologize.

1706   "Afflicted girl" Ann Putnam apologizes for her part in the witch panic.

TIMELINE

1692

January Reverend Parris's young daughter and niece start acting strangely.

February Three women, including a slave, Tituba, are accused of bewitching Parris's daughter and niece and two other village girls.

1692

May Governor William Phips creates a Court of Oyer and Terminer to hear the growing number of witchcraft cases.

June 10 Bridget Bishop, the first to be tried by the new court, is hanged.

July 19 Five more convicted female witches are hanged in Salem.

August 19 Four men and one woman are hanged as witches.

September 22 Six women and two men are hanged as witches in Salem.

October 29 Governor Phips dissolves the Court of Oyer and Terminer.

1711   The Massachusetts government reverses the sentences of most of those convicted in the Salem trials and provides compensation to their families.

2001   Massachusetts governor Jane Swift signs a bill exonerating five men and women executed as witches in 1692 whose sentences had not been reversed in 1711.

1693

January–May The Massachusetts Superior Court, after disallowing spectral evidence, tries 31 accused witches but convicts just 3 of them.

May The witchcraft trials end when Phips orders the release of all accused witches from prison.

1693 ═══════════════ **1711**

1711
The Massachusetts government reverses the sentences of most of those convicted in the Salem trials and provides compensation to their families.

NOTES

CHAPTER 1

1. Quoted in Marilynne K. Roach, *The Salem Witchcraft Trials: A Day-by-Day Chronicle of a Community Under Siege.* New York: First Cooper Square Press, 2002, p. 18.
2. Larry Dale Gragg, *The Salem Witchcraft Crisis.* New York: Praeger, 1992, p. 1.

CHAPTER 2

1. Exodus 22: 18. *The King James Version of the Bible.*
2. Deuteronomy 18: 10–11. *The King James Version of the Bible.*
3. K. David Goss, *The Salem Witchcraft Trials: A Reference Guide.* Westport, Conn.: Greenwood Press, 2008, p. 2.
4. John Demos, *The Enemy Within: 2,000 Years of Witch-Hunting in the Western World.* New York: Viking, 2008, p. 5.
5. Goss, *The Salem Witchcraft Trials,* p. 3.
6. Gragg, *The Salem Witchcraft Crisis,* p. 9.
7. Gragg, *The Salem Witchcraft Crisis,* p. 9.
8. Demos, *The Enemy Within,* p. 39.
9. Quoted in Robert Thurston, *The Witch Hunts: A History of the Witch Persecutions in Europe and North America.* Harlow, UK: Pearson Longman, 2007, p. 99.
10. Thurston, *The Witch Hunts,* p. 65.
11. Demos, *The Enemy Within,* p. 44.
12. Quoted in Thurston, *The Witch Hunts,* p. 65.
13. Thomas L. Purvis, *Colonial America to 1763.* New York: Facts On File, 1999, p. 314.
14. Purvis, *Colonial America,* p. 315.
15. Quoted in Francis J. Bremer, *The Puritan Experiment: New England Society from Bradford to Edwards.* New York: St. Martin's Press, 1976, p. 37.

CHAPTER 3

1. Demos, *The Enemy Within,* p. 215.
2. Frances Hill, *The Salem Witchcraft Trials Reader.* New York: Da Capo Press, 2000, p. 25.
3. Quoted in Demos, *The Enemy Within,* p. 212.
4. Quoted in Paul Boyer and Stephen Nissenbaum, *Salem Possessed: The Social Origins of Witchcraft.* Cambridge, Mass.: Harvard University Press, 1974, p. 45.
5. Quoted in Boyer and Nissenbaum, *Salem Possessed,* p. 58.
6. Gragg, *The Salem Witchcraft Crisis,* p. 34.
7. Boyer and Nissenbaum, *Salem Possessed,* pp. 168–169.
8. Quoted in Hill, *The Salem Witchcraft Trials Reader,* p. 11.

CHAPTER 4

1. Quoted in Boyer and Nissenbaum, *Salem Possessed,* p. 2.
2. Gail Collins, *America's Women: 400 Years of Dolls, Drudges, Helpmates, and Heroines.* New York: HarperCollins, 2003, p. 36.

3. Quoted in Hill, *The Salem Witchcraft Trials Reader*, p. 59.
4. Bernard Rosenthal, *Salem Story: Reading the Witchcraft Trials of 1692*. New York: Cambridge University Press, 1993, p. 2.
5. Quoted in Rosenthal, *Salem Story*, p. 3.
6. Quoted in Roach, *The Salem Witchcraft Trials*, p. 18.
7. Quoted in Hill, *The Salem Witchcraft Trials Reader*, p. 69.
8. Quoted in Goss, *The Salem Witchcraft Trials*, p. 15.
9. Mary Beth Norton, *In the Devil's Snare: The Salem Witchcraft Crisis of 1692*. New York: Alfred A. Knopf, 2002, p. 10.
10. Collins, *America's Women*, p. 36.
11. Boyer and Nissenbaum, *Salem Possessed*, p. 2.
12. Roach, *The Salem Witchcraft Trials*, p. 18.
13. Quoted in Rosenthal, *Salem Story*, p. 26.
14. Demos, *The Enemy Within*, p. 118.
15. Quoted in Gragg, *The Salem Witchcraft Crisis*, p. 48.
16. Quoted in Roach, *The Salem Witchcraft Trials*, p. 25.
17. Quoted in Gragg, *The Salem Witchcraft Crisis*, p. 48.
18. Quoted in Roach, *The Salem Witchcraft Trials*, p. 26.
19. Quoted in Roach, *The Salem Witchcraft Trials*, p. 27.
20. Quoted in Gragg, *The Salem Witchcraft Crisis*, p. 51.
21. Demos, *The Enemy Within*, p. 161.
22. Demos, *The Enemy Within*, p. 161.
23. Quoted in Roach, *The Salem Witchcraft Trials*, p. 29.

CHAPTER 5
1. Quoted in Gragg, *The Salem Witchcraft Crisis*, p. 69.
2. Quoted in Demos, *The Enemy Within*, p. 143.
3. Quoted in Roach, *The Salem Witchcraft Trials*, p. 50.
4. Gragg, *The Salem Witchcraft Crisis*, p. 126.
5. Quoted in Roach, *The Salem Witchcraft Trials*, p. 35.
6. Frances Hill, *A Delusion of Satan: The Full Story of the Salem Witchcraft Trials*. New York: Doubleday, 1995, p. 295.
7. Quoted in Hill, *A Delusion of Satan*, p. 296.
8. Boyer and Nissenbaum, *Salem Possessed*, p. 6.
9. Bremer, *The Puritan Experiment*, p. 165.
10. Quoted in Gragg, *The Salem Witchcraft Crisis*, p. 76.
11. Quoted in Goss, *The Salem Witchcraft Trials*, p. 86.
12. Quoted in Goss, *The Salem Witchcraft Trials*, p. 86.
13. Gragg, *The Salem Witchcraft Crisis*, p. 92.
14. Quoted in Gragg, *The Salem Witchcraft Crisis*, p. 95.

CHAPTER 6
1. Demos, *The Enemy Within*, p. 172.
2. Quoted in Gragg, *The Salem Witchcraft Crisis*, p. 101.
3. Quoted in Demos, *The Enemy Within*, p. 172.
4. Quoted in Hill, *A Delusion of Satan*, p. 164.
5. Quoted in Rosenthal, *Salem Story*, p. 69.
6. Quoted in Gragg, *The Salem Witchcraft Crisis*, p. 102.

7. Hill, *A Delusion of Satan*, p. 164.
8. Quoted in Hill, *A Delusion of Satan*, p. 165.
9. Hill, *A Delusion of Satan*, p. 165.
10. Quoted in Demos, *The Enemy Within*, p. 151.
11. Quoted in Gragg, *The Salem Witchcraft Crisis*, p.153.
12. Quoted in Demos, *The Enemy Within*, p. 174.
13. Quoted in Norton, *In the Devil's Snare*, p. 229.
14. Quoted in Demos, *The Enemy Within*, p. 173.
15. Quoted in Hill, *A Delusion of Satan*, p. 175.
16. Quoted in Gragg, *The Salem Witchcraft Crisis*, p 154.
17. Quoted in Rosenthal, *Salem Story*, p. 145.
18. Demos, *The Enemy Within*, p. 176.

CHAPTER 7

1. Quoted in Norton, *In the Devil's Snare*, p. 275.
2. Quoted in Hill, *A Delusion of Satan*, p. 187.
3. Quoted in Gragg, *The Salem Witchcraft Crisis*, p. 151.
4. Quoted in Demos, *The Enemy Within*, p. 179.
5. Hill, *A Delusion of Satan*, p. 186.
6. Quoted Demos, *The Enemy Within*, p. 179.
7. Hill, *A Delusion of Satan*, p. 189.
8. Quoted in Gragg, *The Salem Witchcraft Crisis*, p. 171.

9. Quoted in Rosenthal, *Salem Story*, p. 136.
10. Demos, *The Enemy Within*, p. 180.
11. Norton, *In the Devil's Snare*, p. 10.
12. Quoted in Demos, *The Enemy Within*, p. 180.
13. Quoted in Rosenthal, *Salem Story*, p. 194.

CHAPTER 8

1. Demos, *The Enemy Within*, p. 185.
2. Hill, *The Salem Witchcraft Trials Reader*, p. 214.
3. Quoted in Demos, *The Enemy Within*, p. 187.
4. Quoted in Roach, *The Salem Witchcraft Trials*, p. 556.
5. Quoted in Demos, *The Enemy Within*, p. 187.
6. Quoted in Roach , *The Salem Witchcraft Trials*, pp. 556–557.
7. Hill, *The Salem Witchcraft Trials Reader*, p. 209.
8. Quoted in Norton, *In the Devil's Snare*, p. 312.
9. Quoted in Roach, *The Salem Witchcraft Trials*, pp. 568–569.
10. Quoted in Hill, *The Salem Witchcraft Trials Reader*, p. 205.
11. Quoted in Demos, *The Enemy Within*, p. 228.
12. Rosenthal, *Salem Story*, p. 1.
13. Boyer and Nissenbaum, Salem *Possessed*, p. 180.
14. Rosenthal, *Salem Story*, p. 3.

BIBLIOGRAPHY

Boyer, Paul, and Stephen Nissenbaum. *Salem Possessed: The Social Origins of Witchcraft*. Cambridge, Mass.: Harvard University Press, 1974.

Bremer, Francis J. *The Puritan Experiment: New England Society from Bradford to Edwards*. New York: St. Martin's Press, 1976.

Collins, Gail. *America's Women: 400 Years of Dolls, Drudges, Helpmates, and Heroines*. New York: HarperCollins, 2003, p. 36.

Demos, John. *The Enemy Within: 2,000 Years of Witch-Hunting in the Western World*. New York: Viking, 2008.

Goss, K. David. *The Salem Witchcraft Trials: A Reference Guide*. Westport, Conn.: Greenwood Press, 2008.

Gragg, Larry Dale. *The Salem Witchcraft Crisis*. New York: Praeger, 1992.

Hill, Frances. *A Delusion of Satan: The Full Story of the Salem Witchcraft Trials*. New York: Doubleday, 1995.

———. *The Salem Witchcraft Trials Reader*. New York: Da Capo Press, 2000.

LaPlante, Eve. *Salem Witch Judge: The Life and Repentance of Samuel Sewall*. New York: HarperOne, 2007.

Norton, Mary Beth. *In the Devil's Snare: The Salem Witchcraft Crisis of 1692*. New York: Alfred A. Knopf, 2002.

Purvis, Thomas L. *Colonial America to 1763*. New York: Facts On File, 1999.

Roach, Marilynne K. *The Salem Witchcraft Trials: A Day-by-Day Chronicle of a Community Under Siege*. New York: First Cooper Square Press, 2002.

Rosenthal, Bernard. *Salem Story: Reading the Witchcraft Trials of 1692.* New York: Cambridge University Press, 1993.

Thurston, Robert. *The Witch Hunts: A History of the Witch Persecutions in Europe and North America.* Harlow, United Kingdom: Pearson Longman, 2007.

FURTHER READING

Aronson, Marc. *Witch-hunt: Mysteries of the Salem Witchcraft Trials.* New York: Atheneum Books, 2003.

Asirvatham, Sandy. *The Salem Witchcraft Trials.* New York: Chelsea House, 2002.

Hill, Frances. *The Salem Witchcraft Trials Reader.* New York: Da Capo Press, 2000.

Kallen, Stuart A. *Figures of the Salem Witchcraft Trials.* Detroit: Lucent, 2005.

Wilson, Lori Lee. *The Salem Witchcraft Trials.* Minneapolis: Lerner, 1997.

WEB SITES

Famous American Trials: Salem Witchcraft Trials 1692

http://www.law.umkc.edu/faculty/projects/ftrials/salem/salem.htm

This account of the witchcraft trials is part of a series on celebrated American trials by Professor Douglas Linder. It includes a chronology, bibliography, images, and primary source materials as well as a detailed analysis of the trials.

Salem Witchcraft Hysteria

http://www.nationalgeographic.com/salem/

This interactive Web site allows students to experience what it was like to be tried as a witch during the Salem witchcraft panic.

Salem Witchcraft Trials

http://salemwitchtrials.com

The site includes a wide selection of information on the trials as well as travel tips for visiting the Salem area and an interactive, online quiz on the witchcraft crisis.

Salem Witchcraft Trials: Documentary Archive and Transcription Project

http://www2.iath.virginia.edu/salem/17docs.html

This extensive collection of primary documents on the Salem witchcraft crisis includes transcripts of the pretrial hearings, historical maps of Salem Village, and biographical sketches of notable people associated with the episode.

Photo Credits

INDEX

A

Abenaki tribe, 21-23
Alden, John, 76
Alden, Priscilla Mullins, 76
Allen, William, 43-44
America
   colonies, 14-15, 21, 73
   culture and society, 4
   history, 2-3, 31, 59, 88, 93,
      98-99
   writers, 72
Andover, Massachusetts
   witch hunt, 68-69
Andros, Edmund, 20-21, 52, 56
Anglican Church, 15-16, 20-21

B

Ballard, Joseph, 68
Barbados, 26-27
Bayley, James, 25
Bibber, Sarah
   victim, 45
Bible
   witchcraft in, 5, 12
Bishop, Bridget
   execution, 59-60, 63, 68, 98
   trial, 58-59, 64, 83
Boston, 55, 68, 72-73, 76, 81,
   92
   harbor, 54
   jails in, 49, 51-52, 54, 58, 69,
      85
   witchcraft in, 15, 20-23, 27-28,
      30-31, 33, 84
Boyer, Paul, 52
   Salem Possessed, 99
Bradbury, Mary, 76
Bradbury, Thomas, 76
Brattle, Thomas, 81

Bremer, Francis, 54
Burroughs, George, 25
   accused witch, 49, 69-72
   trial and conviction, 69-70,
      72-75, 83

C

Calef, Robert, 73-74, 79
   *More Wonders of the Invisible
      World*, 96
Calvin, John, 16
Canada, 21-22, 54, 57
Carrier, Martha, 69
*Cases of Conscience Concerning
   Evil Spirits Personating Men*
   (Mather, I.), 82-83, 97
Catholic church
   leaders, 6, 8-9, 15-16
   and witchcraft, 5-6, 8
Charles I, King of England, 20
Charles II, King of England, 20
Cheever, Ezekiel, 40
Christianity
   leaders, 6, 16, 23
   and witchcraft, 5-6, 8, 13
Cloyce, Sarah
   accused witch, 46, 48-49, 85
   arrest, 46, 48, 79
   specters, 49
Cold War, 100
Collins, Gail, 33, 36
Connecticut, 18
Corey, Giles
   accused witch, 49, 51
   death, 77-78
Corey, Martha, 76
   accused witch, 46, 48-49, 77
   arrest, 46-47
   death, 79

Corwin, Jonathan
    judge, 56
    questioning of the witches, 38,
        40, 47, 57
Cotton, John, 72
Court of Oyer and Terminer,
    79
    creation of, 54-57, 77
    criticism of, 81-83
    first session, 58-61, 63
    second session, 64-68
    September trials, 75-77
    suspension of, 84-85, 92-93
    third session, 68-72
Courtship of Miles Standish, The
    (Longfellow), 76
Crucible, The (Miller), 100

D
Danforth, Thomas, 49, 85
Demos, John
    historian, 8, 10-11, 23, 38,
        42-43, 60, 67-68, 74, 83-84,
        90
Discourse of the Damned Art of
    Witchcraft, A (Perkins), 12
Dudley, Joseph, 98

E
Eames, Rebecca, 76
Eastey, Mary, 85
    accused witch, 49, 76
    arrest, 49, 79
    death, 79
    petition of, 79-80
England, 57, 72, 92
    colonists, 14, 26
    Glorious Revolution in, 21
    government, 15, 20-21,
        52-53
    religion in, 16, 20-21
    witch hunts in, 9-10
English, Mary
    accused witch, 50, 76

English, Philip
    accused witch, 50-51, 61, 76
Essay for the Recording of Illustri-
    ous Providences, An (Mather, I.),
    28, 30-31
Europe, 73
    religion in, 8
    society and culture, 11
    witchcraft in, 6, 8-14, 30

F
Faulkner, Abigail, 76, 85, 96
Fisk, Thomas, 91
Foster, Ann, 76
France, 21, 57, 91, 99

G
Gallows Hill, 59, 67, 70, 72, 96
Gedney, Bartholomew
    judge, 56
Gerrish, Joseph, 85
Glover, Goodwife, 31
Good, Dorcas
    accused witch, 45
    arrest, 45, 51-52
    specter, 51
Good, Sarah
    accused witch, 38-40, 42-43,
        45
    arrest, 38, 44, 51, 58, 88
    interrogation, 39-40, 42
    specter, 40, 43-44
    trial and conviction, 64,
        67-68
Good, William, 40, 42, 52
Goodwin bewitchment, 28-29,
    33-35
Goodwin, John, 28, 31, 33, 35
Goss, K. David, 6
Gould, Benjamin, 49
Gragg, Larry, 2, 9, 27, 51, 59
Gray, Samuel, 59
Green, Joseph, 95
Griggs, William, 35-36

H

Hale, John, 32-33, 85
   A Modest Enquiry into the
     Nature of Witchcraft, 94, 96
Hathorne, Jonathan
   judge, 56, 94
   questioning of the witches,
     38, 40, 42, 44-45, 47, 57
Hawthorne, Nathaniel
   The House of Seven Gables,
     94
Herrick, Mary, 85
Henry VIII, King of England, 15
Hill, Frances
   historian, 23, 28, 51, 78-79,
     91, 94
Hoar, Dorcas, 76
Hobbs, Abigail, 76
   confession, 65-67, 81
Hobbs, Deliverance
   confession, 65-67
House of Seven Gables, The
   (Hawthorne), 94
Howe, Elizabeth, 64
Hubbard, Elizabeth
   bewitching, 36-37, 40, 42
   fits, 40, 42
Hughes, John, 43-44
Hull, Hannah, 92
Hutchinson, Thomas, 35

I

Ingersoll, Nathaniel, 38-39
Innocent VIII, Pope, 6
Ipswich, Massachusetts, 49, 51

J

Jacobs, George
   accused witch, 49
   trial and conviction, 69-70
Jacobs, Margaret, 69-70
James II, King of England,
   20-21, 52, 56

Jewish religion
   and witchcraft, 5-6
John Indian, 37, 48
Johnson, Elizabeth Jr., 85

K

Keene, Paula, 98
King William's War, 21-22, 24
Knapp, Elizabeth, 30
Kramer, Heinrich
   Malleus Maleficarum, 6-10

L

Lacy, Mary, 76
LaPlante, Eve, 92
Lawson, Deodat, 25
Lewis, Mercy, 45, 59, 64
Lilly, Jane, 76
Longfellow, Henry Wadsworth
   The Courtship of Miles
     Standish, 76

M

Maine, 21-23, 84
Malleus Maleficarum (Kramer
   and Sprenger)
   guidelines in, 6-10
Martin, Susannah, 64
Massachusetts, 1-2, 4, 9, 27, 38
   charter, 21, 23, 52, 54
   government, 16, 19-22, 29,
     52-54, 56-57, 60-61, 63, 70,
     81, 84, 86, 88, 91-93, 96-99
   military, 21-23, 29, 54
   settlements in, 15-16
   society in, 18-21, 61, 72, 76, 88
   witchcraft in, 30, 33, 35, 51, 70
Mather, Cotton
   influence of, 23, 58, 60, 70,
     72, 74, 97
   Memorable Providences,
     Relating to Witchcrafts and
     Possessions, 28, 30-31, 33-34

smallpox vaccine, 73
The Wonders of the Invisible World, 83-84, 97
Mather, Increase
    Cases of Conscience Concerning Evil Spirits Personating Men, 82-83, 97
    An Essay for the Recording of Illustrious Providences, 28, 30-31
    influence of, 53-54, 60, 69, 81, 83-84
    Return of Several Ministers, 81
McCarthy, Joseph, 99-100
Melijn, Jacob, 68
Memorable Providences, Relating to Witchcrafts and Possessions (Mather, C.), 28, 30-31, 33-34
Middle East, 5-6, 11-12, 43
Miller, Arthur
    The Crucible, 100
Misogyny, 10, 12
Modest Enquiry into the Nature of Witchcraft, A (Hale), 94, 96

N
Native American tribes, 21-23, 91, 93, 99
New England, 78, 81
    colonies, 15-16, 21, 24
    economy in, 19
    history of, 18-19
    politics in, 19
    Puritans in, 12, 15, 17, 23, 52, 58, 72, 83-84
    witchcraft in, 2-3, 15, 17-18, 38, 46-47, 51, 98
New Hampshire, 22-23
Newton, Thomas, 58
New York, 14
Nissenbaum, Stephen, 52
    Salem Possessed, 99

Norton, Mary Beth, 36, 84
Noyes, Nicholas, 68, 79
Nurse, Rebecca, 85
    accused witch, 46, 48-49, 61, 66
    arrest, 46, 48, 58, 66, 79
    specter, 48-49
    supporters, 66, 89, 91
    trial and conviction, 64, 66-67, 91
Nurse, Samuel, 91

O
Osborne, Alexander, 38, 42
Osborne, Sarah
    accused witch, 38-40, 42-43, 45
    arrest, 38, 44, 51
    death, 51
    interrogation, 39, 42
    poor health, 42
    scandalous past, 38, 42
    specter, 43-44

P
Parker, Alice, 76
    death, 79
Parker, Mary, 76
    death, 79
Parris, Betty, 48
    mysterious fits, 1-2, 32-37, 40, 42
Parris, Samuel, 38, 42, 87
    apology, 89-91, 94
    congregation, 32, 48
    minister, 1-2, 25-29, 31, 36-37, 47-48, 89-90
    resignation, 91
    witchcraft beliefs, 35, 58
Pennsylvania, 14
Perkins, William
    A Discourse of the Damned Art of Witchcraft, 12

Phillips, Abigail, 72
Phips, Mary Spencer, 84
Phips, William, 22
  governor, 54, 56, 60-61, 67,
    69, 79, 84-87, 89, 96
  military, 54, 56-57
Pilgrims, 15-17
Plymouth Colony, 15-16
Post, Mary, 85
Proctor, Elizabeth, 65-66
  accused witch, 46, 48-49
  arrest, 46, 58
  release, 70, 96
  specter, 49
  trial and conviction, 69-70,
    85
Proctor, John, 65-66
  accused witch, 49, 51
  arrest, 58
  trial and conviction, 69
Proctor, John Jr., 70
Proctor, William, 69
Protestant
  religious movement, 8-9,
    15-16, 20
Pudeator, Ann, 76, 79
Puritans
  clergy, 12, 33, 37, 57, 58, 60-61,
    72, 81
  fear, 19, 48
  leaders, 12, 15, 20, 26, 31, 52
  legal code, 21
  native land, 9
  new world mission, 15-18
  religious beliefs, 15-16, 25
  revolution, 20
  settlers, 20
  threats to, 23
  and witchcraft, 2, 15, 30, 91
Purvis, Thomas, 14-15
Putnam, Ann
  apology, 94-96
  bewitching, 36, 38, 45, 59

  claims, 37, 47, 51, 64-65, 70,
    94
  fits, 40, 42, 47
Putnam, Ann Sr.
  victim, 45, 48
Putnam, Edward, 38
Putnam, Thomas, 36, 38, 70, 89

R

Redd, Wilmott, 76
  death, 79
Reformation, 8
Return of Several Ministers
  (Mather, I.), 81
Revolutionary War, 98
Richards, John
  judge, 56-57, 85
Roach, Marilynne, 37
Rosenthal, Bernard, 34, 98

S

Salem Possessed (Boyer and
  Nissenbaum), 99
Salem Village, Massachusetts, 1,
  5, 23
  conspiracy in, 27-32
  economy, 24-25, 27
  factionalism in, 23-25, 29
  fear in, 32, 36, 44, 46-47,
    99-100
  persecutions, 4, 15, 17, 19,
    24-25, 28, 31, 89
  separatists in, 27
  society in, 2-3, 18, 24-28,
    35-40, 42, 49, 55, 70, 91, 99
  traditionalists in, 25
  trials in, 34-35, 43, 46-61,
    64-66, 69, 72-73, 75-88,
    91-92, 95, 97-98, 100
Salem Town, Massachusetts, 48
  community, 24, 27, 35, 38,
    49-50, 68, 89
  economy, 27

jails in, 49, 51-52, 54, 85
  trials in, 58, 69, 76, 91
Saltonstall, Nathaniel
  judge, 56-57, 64
Satan, 16
  agents of, 2, 6, 8-9, 13-14, 23,
    30, 43, 48, 61, 74, 83, 91
  book, 81
  influence, 12, 17, 32, 38, 61-63,
    83, 96
Scott, Margaret, 76
  death, 79
Separatists, 16
Sergeant, Peter
  judge, 56
Sewall, Samuel
  apology, 93-94
  judge, 56, 85, 91-94
Sheldon, Susannah, 45
Sibley, Mary, 37
Sprague, Martha, 76
Sprenger, Jacob
  Malleus Maleficarum, 6-10
Stoughton, William
  judge, 55-57, 59, 64, 67, 69,
    85-86, 94
  lieutenant governor, 54-57,
    63, 83
Superior Court of Judicature,
  84, 86-87, 92
supernatural, 2
  possessions, 36
  powers, 6, 31
Swift, Jane, 98

T

Taylor, Mary, 76
Tertullian, 13
Thurston, Robert, 10
Tituba, 48
  accused witch, 37-38, 42
  arrest, 38, 44, 66, 87
  confession, 42-46, 65-66, 81, 87

questioning of, 42-45
  release, 87
  specter, 37, 44
Topsfield, Massachusetts, 49,
  64-65, 76

V

Virginia, 14

W

Walcott, Mary, 45
Wardwell, Samuel
  death, 79
  trial and conviction, 76-77
Wardwell, Sarah, 77, 85
Warren, Mary, 45
  confession, 65-66
Wildes, Sarah, 64
Willard, John, 69
Willard, Samuel, 81, 83
William and Mary of Orange,
  21, 52
Williams, Abigail, 64
  claims, 40, 48, 64-65
  mysterious fits, 1-2, 32-35,
    37, 42, 59
Winthrop, John, 16
Winthrop, Wait
  judge, 56, 85
witchcraft
  accusers, 10, 13-14, 35-36, 40,
    42-43, 47-49, 51, 59, 64-66,
    76-77
  characteristics, 12-14
  confessions, 8, 42-46, 65-68,
    70, 76-77, 80-81, 85
  craze, 24-25, 54, 58, 60, 68-70,
    75, 77, 82, 89, 94, 98-100
  cults, 7-9, 43, 65, 70
  and devil worship, 2, 8-10,
    12-14, 17, 30, 35, 46
  dolls, 58-59
  early history, 5-15

escapees, 76
evil deeds of, 7-8, 10, 48-49,
  56, 59, 64
executions, 9, 14-15, 17-18,
  31, 59-60, 64, 66-70, 72-73,
  75-79, 81, 83, 85-86, 88,
  96-99
female, 10-13
hunts, 2-4, 6, 8-9, 15, 19,
  30-31, 38, 47-49, 51-52, 58,
  60, 65, 67-68, 89, 94
laws, 14

punishment, 3, 8, 12-13,
  17-18
statutes, 14-15
testing procedure, 8, 37-39,
  43-45, 49, 52, 61-64, 67
trials, 3-4, 6, 8-11, 13-15, 17,
  19, 28, 30-31, 47-73, 75-88,
  91-95, 99-100
victims, 28-29, 31, 45, 64, 76,
  88, 97
*Wonders of the Invisible World,
The* (Mather, C.), 83-84, 97